Money isn't easy. Marriage isn't eas

two, chaos is often the result. *Your Money, Your Marriage* will clear up the chaos, get you on the same page as your spouse, and most importantly, improve your relationship. Brian and Cherie Lowe do a great job of being vulnerable and transparent, while also providing you a treasure map to a successful marriage.

Peter Dunn, Pete the Planner, personal finance expert, *USA Today* columnist, radio and television personality

America is in a period of unprecedented darkness during which many married couples are struggling to survive. In such a moment, I cannot think of a more needed book than *Your Money, Your Marriage*. The Lowes offer a combination of inspiring principles and practical tools in a book that is superbly written. This book has the power to save your marriage if it is hurting or strengthen your marriage if it is healthy. If you long for a deepened intimacy and secure financial future, read this now. It's a flash of light in a dark world and comes to us not a moment too soon.

Jonathan Merritt, contributing writer for *The Atlantic* and author of *Learning to Speak God from Scratch*

Invest in your marriage by reading this book! Cherie and Brian offer smart strategies and practical tools through humorous storytelling.

Margaret Feinberg, author of *Flourish*

Speaking from personal experience, there is no bigger source of conflict for couples than money! I love how Brian and Cherie open up their lives to encourage and empower couples to get on the same page about money, and improve their intimacy in the process!

Ruth Soukup, *New York Times* bestselling author of *Living Well, Spending Less* and *Unstuffed*

This book is powerful because it combats the areas of marriage that are the most vulnerable. In the pages of this book lie incredible truths and practical wisdom that will surely help you transform your marriage and your finances to new levels of harmony.

Talaat and Tai McNeely, founders of His and Her Money

Your Money, Your Marriage

Your Money, Your Marriage

CHERIE AND BRIAN LOWE

ZONDERVAN

Your Money, Your Marriage

Requests for information should be addressed to:
Zondervan, *3900 Sparks Dr. SE, Grand Rapids, Michigan 49546*

ISBN 978-0-310-35122-1 (softcover)

ISBN 978-0-310-35544-1 (audio)

ISBN 978-0-310-35123-8 (ebook)

Author is represented by The Christopher Ferebee Agency, www.christopherferebee.com.

Interior design: Denise Froehlich

First printing July 2018 / Printed in the United States of America

Contents

Introduction

Sex and money.

We can't think of two things that make people go more absolutely crazy or feel more awkward. You only have to flip through *People* magazine, dive to cover your kids' eyes during a movie preview, or even find yourselves bickering about overdraft fees and spending habits to confirm it.

Perhaps we're just gluttons for punishment. Our first book, *Slaying the Debt Dragon,* shared our story of paying off over $127,000 in debt. Spilling our guts about exactly how we first racked up that much debt and then found our way to a financial happily ever after might have shocked some of our friends and family. For us, it was cathartic. Release and true freedom resulted from knowing our journey might help someone else who felt hopeless in their current state of personal finance.

In this book we're taking things one step further and frankly talking about the strong connection between sex and money—in our marriage and in yours. If you never contemplated the link between your finances and intimacy before, we can promise you they hold hands every single second of the day. Just think about the last fight you and your spouse had about money. Did it end in a night of hot passion? Um, yeah, that's a negative.

In a culture riddled with divorce, where the top reasons for ending it all involve, you guessed it, sex and money, how can a couple even pray to make it to "until death do us part" when couples really mean "until debt do us part"?

We have learned, however, that the better we manage money as a couple, the closer we draw together in other ways too (insert "bow, chicka, wow, wow" here since we clearly have the sense of humor of fifteen-year-olds). This led us to a big what-if dream.

What if we . . .

- explained how couples can get on the same page about money?
- opened an honest discussion about what it's really like for husbands and wives to balance a household budget and stay married?
- helped couples overcome that initial awkwardness of communicating about and managing money together?
- shared our successes and mistakes to help other couples gain restored hope for both their finances and their relationships?
- talked about how our attitudes toward spending, saving, games of comparison, and hopes for the future neatly mesh into how things work in every area of marriage?
- pushed back against a culture that confuses desire with commitment and lust with marital intimacy?

Through our own experience—and through research—we discovered that the way you approach your money spills over into every aspect of your marriage, including the bedroom. So we decided to explore that very concept with you and share a bit of our experience.

Best of all, we mutually agreed to this crazy idea of lending both of our voices to this book, so you could get honest opinions and ideas from a husband and a wife who live this stuff every day. We're far from perfect people, but we're always happy to open up our lives if it might encourage one person or enrich one marriage or change one financial relationship—providing more intimacy and an abundant life.

Because of this unique format and style of authorship, we'll do our best to provide obvious road signs along the way. Some portions of the book we wrote together. We literally sat on the couch next to each other—working in Google Docs—taking no small amount of pleasure correcting each other's grammar and inserting inappropriate comments, only to have them deleted by the other.

Sections of the text have been written by Brian, who brings not only his unique perspective as a husband but also over fifteen years of experience as a divorce lawyer. He knows what can land you in his office, seeking to end your marriage, and which practices can safeguard your relationship to protect against divorce. He also has a vast knowledge of 1980s movies and professional wrestling, both always certain to pop up when he explains something. You'll be hearing from Cherie too. She will share what she's experienced as Brian's wife and a number of stories encountered in the past ten years of being a personal finance author and blogger.

But our heart and prayer for *Your Money, Your Marriage* really isn't about either one of us or our relationship. It's about you. We long for your marriage to grow stronger and happier. We wish for you and your spouse to experience deepened intimacy and flourishing finances. We ache for you to avoid the mistakes we've made when it comes to money and marriage. And more than anything, we yearn for you to realize there is always hope. Your marriage is not over; your financial situation is not beyond repair.

In each chapter, you will find specific exercises to help further that hope for your finances and your relationship. If you're reading this book with your spouse or a small group, those questions and projects should be done together. If you're flying solo, please don't skip over these sections. They were designed with you in mind too. And the simple, intentional practice of evaluating your attitudes, habits, and experiences will be of great use. You might even learn a new thing or two about yourself.

We can't promise some of our words won't make you blush a little. But we can promise if you show up in your relationship, make efforts toward changing your attitudes and habits when it comes to both money and marriage, and pray like your lives count on it, intimacy will blossom like never before. And that's when the real fun begins (insert winky face here).

CHAPTER 1

Origin Stories

In my beginning is my end.

T. S. ELIOT

Where you begin matters.

Your first breath, your first steps, your hometown, your first job—before you even realize it, every single "first" begins to determine who you will become. You get more than just a warm fuzzy when you consider where you started. You gain strength from your beginnings.

Great power abounds where your relationship began. Years of conflict and the plain ol' wear and tear of day-to-day life can erode that terrific force. Whispers from the enemy of your souls try to convince you that the burgeoning of your relationship doesn't count anymore. It's a page in your history, long-forgotten and unimportant.

But beginnings *do* matter. Making a regular practice of recounting your marriage's origin story can return you to that terrific force.

Perhaps dusty and dormant, those wild emotions of love and attraction once knit you tightly together, intertwining your hearts, souls, and hands. That same beginning catapulted you to a future where your finances—and legs—intertwine too.

In the beginning, God created husband and wife, and it was beautiful. It was very good. In the beginning, God created your marriage and it, too, was beautiful. It, too, was very good. Bring the memory of that beauty, of that goodness, to the forefront of your mind and believe that what began as something good can be something great.

The Fifth House on the Right: Brian

"At the T intersection, you're gonna make a left, and it will be the fifth house on the right."

Unequivocally, those were the greatest directions I've ever received. Eh-ver. Once upon a time, before Cherie and I walked the aisle, we were two bright-eyed college students full of promise and hope. She was beautiful. I was persistent. She was brilliant. I was smitten. Long before we vanquished foes together, long before our war against the debt dragon, we broke bread together—for the first time. That story begins with the "fifth house on the right."

On the evening of our first date, your dashing protagonist (creative liberty) traversed to a distant and unknown land. Because it was a long journey—seriously, it was far—and he didn't know the terrain, your protagonist needed the aforesaid directions: "It will be the fifth house on the right." These weren't suburban "close to each other, population-dense neighborhood" houses. These were "slow down to fifty miles an hour and still be effective at counting" houses. Experts refer to the distance between these homes as a "fer piece." Corn grows tall and basketball rims adorn old wooden barns in this land.

At the T, there's a sign that marks the junction of two state highways. I stopped as instructed. In that moment, I didn't know I was picking up my future bride. I didn't know the significance that junction sign would play less than a year later. I didn't know my life was about to exponentially improve. I didn't know those were the last directions that would ever really matter. All I knew is that I needed to make a left turn and start counting: 1, 2, 3, 4, 5.

Cherie's folks still live in the fifth house on the right. I still count those houses. I still feel the anticipation. I still feel overwhelming joy every time we visit. There's a new house en route that gets skipped in the count, because moments, memories, and places of significance transcend "math."

Defining statements compose life's symphony. We all have statements that have changed the course of our lives. When she said "Yes," when she said "I do," when I heard "It's a girl" and "You passed"—these were all game changer statements in my life. For me though, everything else occurring thereafter is predicated on the fifth-house directions and everything preceding was a prelude thereto. I'm forever thankful I followed those directions. I'd make that left turn and count all over again. And again.

Maybe you need some direction. Maybe you need to start with a game changer statement about your money and your marriage. Look at your spouse and say, "I am for you, I am with you, I choose you." Share a vision for a better marriage, for a better financial future. Words have power. Use words to build up one another. Use words to direct each other to a better tomorrow. Use words to love one another. You are always on the precipice of a new journey, at the foot of an origin story. Whatever it looks like for you, make the left turn and start counting.

When I Fall in Love: Cherie

Before Tinder or match.com, Brian and I fell in love online. We had a long-distance relationship enhanced by dial-up internet. While my parents lived only thirty minutes away from Brian, I attended a small college over five hours from him. After a whirlwind summer romance, I returned to finish my senior year. In the olden days, before Wi-Fi, if someone picked up the phone, interrupting that screechy noise from the modem, you would cut them. Brian and I primarily communicated by email, but when we eventually upped our tech skills, we also crushed on AOL Instant Messenger. For our first Valentine's Day, Brian printed out two large volumes of all the messages we ever wrote to each other and then had them bound. Still a treasure, I recently dusted them off to read the beginning of our story.

In two hot minutes of reading our story, I realized two things: (1) Brian was working hard to pitch game. (2) He enjoyed writing me within the email I had just sent him—which at first makes them a little difficult to read, but once you get the hang of it, you can actually "hear" the conversation.

Without further ado, the first email message I ever received from the charming rascal I would eventually marry:

B: What's goin' down, Cherie?

How romantic is this opening sentence? It's obvious why I fell head over heels for him. Young men, take note.

C: Just thought I would drop you a quick line. I really can't believe we bumped into each other again. So funny—funny strange, not funny ha-ha.

We really did physically bump into one another. I had just been telling a friend about a boy I once worked with at JCPenney but hadn't seen in years. I walked into JCPenney and plowed directly into him. Neither of us worked there anymore, and I have no idea why he was in the Juniors' department. It's an even crazier story than it sounds.

B: So you think I'm strange, huh? Just kidding.
Such a conversationalist.

C: Well, I made it back up to Wisconsin. I only have a week and a half of camps left here before I return to Indiana for a few days and then move on to Kentucky.
I'm not sure why I just spelled out my two-week travel itinerary. During college, I worked for the Salvation Army in Wisconsin over two summer breaks. Yes, I fit the stereotypical camp counselor mold. My parents lived in rural Indiana (and still do), and I was gearing up for my final year of college in Wilmore, Kentucky, just outside of Lexington. I was literally "Just a small-town girl, livin' in a lonely world."

B: So give me some dates here, tiger. When are you coming back to Indiana?
*First thought: *blush* he called me tiger. Second thought: he can't read. I just said a week and a half.*

C: What a crazy life I lead! I can't really believe that I only have a year of college left. I absolutely cannot be this old. And here I stand, trying to decide what I'm going to do with the rest of my life.

Oh, twenty-one-year-old Cherie, you are so cute. Double your age, have two children, and then get back to me about feeling old. Also? I still don't know what I'm going to do with the rest of my life. You're welcome.

B: I feel your pain. Do you get the funny (strange, not ha-ha) feeling that you are going to make or break the entire course of the rest of your life with every decision you make within the next year? Maybe that's just me.

So there you have it—the original "Once Upon a Time" for our story begins with a wee bit of flirting and much fretting over the future. I wish I could give twenty-two-year-old Brian a hug (and not just because I thought he was totally adorable and hot at the same time), letting him know it would all be okay and that maybe he was putting a little too much pressure on himself.

It probably would have freaked out twenty-two-year-old Brian to know that he would make a decision within that year to ask a small-town, red-haired girl who felt so old at twenty-one to marry him. But that's exactly what happened.

Rereading those emails reminded me that twenty-two-year-old Brian and forty-two-year-old Brian still have a lot in common. Both remain simultaneously hot and adorable to me. Both can put too much pressure on the decision-making process. Both are incredible flirts. Sure, Brian has grown and matured over the last twenty years of our relationship, but the things I loved about him the most—his sense of humor, his quirky way of making me giggle like a schoolgirl, and his intense desire to succeed in life—remain unchanged.

I'd hazard a guess that some of the initial feelings you had about your spouse when you first met remain the same too. Even if you don't have hundreds of pages of emails, you do have a beginning. Spend fifteen minutes recalling the first time you bumped into each other. Whether you choose to write out a narrative, write your spouse a letter, or simply share your origin story with one another, do it now.

Side note: we all have differing memories of what we experienced and the minor details of our story. Avoid the temptation to correct your spouse or begin a sentence with "Noooo, that's not what happened!" We're not trying to build a detailed, specific record for the National Archives; we're trying to capture the spirit of why you fell in love with one another.

Need a few sparks to kindle that fire? Answer the following questions:

What were you wearing? What was your spouse wearing?

Where had you been just prior to meeting?

Were you nervous?

What sounds, smells, or sights were there?

Take a few minutes to further examine and evaluate the beginning of your love story. List three character traits you admired or were taken with when you met your spouse and you still value today.

Her:	Him:
1. ____________________	1. ____________________
2. ____________________	2. ____________________
3. ____________________	3. ____________________

Within this short excerpt of the first page of our love story, I can also see some red flags. Twenty-one-year-old Cherie and twenty-two-year-old Brian already display that perhaps they don't always do the best job of communicating with one another. Remember my travel itinerary? It resulted in some playful banter, but gives a brief foreshadowing of future events. Even when I think I'm being clear, my words might not lend a full picture of what I'm trying to say to Brian.

Does this mean I need to find Doc Brown and fire up the DeLorean to warn myself to stay away from this flirtatious fella? Absolutely not. However, being honest about any struggles you had at the beginning of your story provides an opportunity for growth and improvement. Problems within marriages (specifically within the ways couples handle money) don't just materialize overnight. You can see the beginnings of challenges within the beginnings of relationships.

Can we get one thing straight here? Challenges and even conflict within marriage are not bad things. In fact, I'd be kind of terrified if you and your spouse agreed one hundred percent about every single thing in your relationship and the day-to-day management of your family and home. It either means one of you is lying or you're both the offspring of Vicki from the 1980s TV series *Small Wonder.* (In case you're wondering, the little girl who played that robot is now in her forties and is a nurse in Boulder, Colorado.)

When we begin to believe the lie that happy couples don't fight, miscommunicate, or make mistakes, we plant foolish seeds of malcontent in our hearts. Those seedlings, if not plucked from our relationships, lead us further down the road of deception to believing that other people have happier marriages, or even worse, that someone else would make us happier. Once the lie takes root, it takes approximately two seconds for us to arrive at that illogical and erroneous conclusion.

No doubt your early relationship had its challenges, as all relationships do. Maybe you've overcome some of those challenges, or maybe you're still working on them. Maybe you've never even thought about identifying them until now. Again, pause for a moment to think through challenges you had at the beginning of your romance. Did you have a specific hurdle you had to overcome to even make it down the aisle? Was there a great distance between the two of you? Did you fight over something small or miscommunicate in a major way? Were friends and family telling you that you were crazy to marry your spouse?

Great news! You overcame those challenges. Even better news: you can learn from the challenges you once faced and can apply the lessons you learned to new challenges. Life functions in patterns. Once you begin to crack the code of what makes both of you tick, you have greater odds for future success.

One minor word of caution as you move through the exercise of recounting your story. In *Do Over: Rescue Monday, Reinvent Your Work, and Never Get Stuck*, Jon Acuff drops this wisdom: "We love to idealize the past when our present doesn't meet our expectations." It can be easy to remember your "Once Upon a Time" as much more glimmering and exciting than the boring or challenging middle chapters you may find yourself in right now. Don't fall into the trap of treasuring your beginnings over what's happening right now. Each page is essential. Each page overflows with beauty. Each page is part of your story.

Why Your Marriage Needs Dan Henry: Brian

While where you begin is awesome and important, at some point you have to talk about where you're going.

Do you know Dan Henry? I don't either, but I know his work. You've probably seen it too and just didn't realize it was his. Dan Henry invented directional markers for organized bicycle events. They look a little bit like this but are spray-painted on the road:

It doesn't sound or look amazing in print, but think about it. Organized bicycle rides are longer than organized runs, making it more important and more difficult to keep everyone on course—in a literal sense. Without directional guidance, somebody's gonna end up at a dimly lit speakeasy, asking for directions on the wrong side of town. Apparently, when I imagine a bicycle tragedy, it's in a 1920s Prohibition-setting noir.

Enter Dan Henry. His directional signs are painted on the pavement. Not much else decorates the pavement, making the signage conspicuous. The symbols look like utility markers to the unfamiliar eye. But to the cyclist, these symbols protect the path. The markers are called—wait for it—Dan Henrys. Now I'm not sure if Dan was so bold as to name his road signs after himself, but if so, well played, Dan Henry, well played.

Cherie is crazy. I mean that in the most loving way. Crazy-fun is a better way of stating it. For a handful of years in a row, she rode her bicycle 160 miles in one day as part of an organized ride. In July. Once when she was pregnant. Another time when she had shingles. Given her crimson hair and alabaster skin, the fiery July sun is not her friend. But she always kept going. Dan Henry proved invaluable. Without Dan's direction, she might still be out on the course.

Cherie often rode said 160 miles with her friend Holly. The ride is on a state highway, and I would drive back roads or on the interstate to leapfrog around them. Along scheduled stops for hydration, I would meet Cherie and Holly, take their bikes, and hand them towels and water. One particular stop, they were behind pace. I was a little concerned. It turned out a group of other riders had convinced them the route led a different way. The other riders were wrong. It put them eleven miles off course. One hundred seventy-one miles is more than 160. Depending on the time of day, those eleven extra miles of brutal sunshine can take their toll.

My immediate question was, "Are you okay?"

That's not true. That's what my question *should* have been.

My actual question—me, who gets sore after a two-mile bike ride to work—was: "Why didn't you follow the Dan Henrys?"

Too tired to pummel me, Cherie responded: "We did. They were the wrong Dan Henrys."

There had been another race the week before. A different course. A different set of Dan Henrys.

Heads up! Don't follow somebody else's Dan Henrys or follow the wrong examples. You're not going where they're going. You don't want to finish where they finish. Listening to the wrong voices or following the wrong directions leads to nothing but pain in your marriage and failure in your finances.

Oh, how I wish we had known these truths when we were first married. We lacked financial direction. No Dan Henrys. We were smart people, but we made financial decisions based on whim and misinformation as opposed to prudence and God's plan for our lives.

I remember being in a huge, modern lecture hall during law school, surrounded by some of the brightest minds I've ever known. We all took student loan documents and passed them around to the next classmate for signature. At graduation, many of us procured loans to "get by" while we studied for the bar exam. It's difficult now to wrap my brain around why it seemed like a grand idea to borrow money for the express reason of unemployment. But everybody else was doing it, so I followed their example without questioning it.

By taking this advice and following the wrong Dan Henrys, we found ourselves with over $90,000 of student loan debt from college, law school, and the "get by" loan. The catch, of course, is that loans always come due. And then they often domino. Our hefty student loan payment made it difficult to pay for emergency car repairs or medical bills, so we used a credit card. The credit card bill added up quickly and we began charging other purchases too. Of course, I also needed transportation to get to work—work I needed to pay for the loan. The only Dan Henry we saw pointing toward how to buy a vehicle led right into the finance office of the local dealership. Throw in some furniture and more medical bills and we were soon under water to the tune of around $127,000.

You can avoid this "suddenly, somehow" syndrome by discerning the right Dan Henrys for your money and in your marriage. Making a plan in advance is a great a Dan Henry in your marriage or for your money. Dan Henrys aren't painted by cyclists during the ride; they're painted a day or two before, with the proper direction and finish line in mind. Lay out as much of the course as you can before you need it. Protect the path. Having frequent financial discussions protects the path and prevents unwanted detours on the road to financial freedom. You can lay out the course of your marriage by scheduling and enjoying intentional time with your spouse.

We Are Financial Failures (and We're Okay with It): Cherie

My grandma Thelma owned one of the greatest inventions of the 1980s. Part office equipment, part weapon, when I cradled it in my tiny hands, I could create an organized future, perhaps an entire new world. Set on top of the hard plastic handle was a rigid disc with each letter of the alphabet and numbers zero through nine. Select the letter or number of your choice, squeeze the trigger, and—*boom!*—a small plastic sticker emerged from the top. Choose the next letter and before you knew it, you were spelling all of the words. My favorite practice included creating my name and then sticking the rectangular CHERIE tab on an item I owned, returning to the label maker to create yet another.

Labels are weird. As soon as we exit the womb, we begin to amass them. Such a handsome boy! What a pretty girl! He's a fussy baby. She's the perfect angel. As we grow, those labels continue to multiply and are given to us by a number of different people—family members, teachers, friends, neighbors, and the old guy who lives across the street who proclaims, "Get out of my yard, you useless kid! It's my ball now!" We label ourselves too. I'm a straight-A student, a jock, a successful businessperson, a health nut.

We rarely choose to share the labels we're less proud of though. The next time you meet a stranger, I'm guessing you won't open with, "I'm a serial late arriver! If I'm supposed to be at your house at a set time, just count on me showing up thirty minutes late." Or at Meet the Teacher Night, you probably don't exclaim, "I love my kid, but he drives me up the wall, and then I lose my junk yelling at him and make him cry. I feel like a poor excuse for a parent."

Some labels are accurate. I'm a mom. I'm an author. I'm a friend. Some labels—both the ones we give ourselves and the ones handed out by others—are not accurate.

Not too long ago, I sat down with personal finance author and radio personality Pete the Planner to chat over coffee. With numerous books, TV appearances, and a demanding speaking schedule, he's kind of a big deal. But he took a break from his busy schedule to meet with me, and I peppered him with questions about the pursuit of helping others to manage their money well. In the middle of our conversation, he paused to ask me a question I wrestled with for months.

"Do you consider yourself a personal finance expert?"

I quickly answered no to this label question. Because as much as I've learned about paying off debt and saving money, I realize there are plenty of people who are much more intelligent and financially savvy than I.

"I guess I'm a money saving expert?" I replied in an unconvincing tone, unsure if I was trying to persuade him or myself.

A few weeks later I realized how I should have responded. Doesn't that always happen? If I could go back in time, I would have replied in a much more confident tone, "I am a personal finance failure."

As much as I'm thrilled we found a way out of over $127,000 in debt, I frequently remind myself we were the people who acquired that much debt to begin with. There were so many mistakes, so many unwise choices, and so much inattention to our finances. Ours is a story of money and marriage failure as much as it is one of success. Six years after paying off all our debt and working through our issues, I've come to a realization.

I'm okay with being a failure.

These are big words. I'm not one to swiftly admit my faults (however, I'm excellent at pointing them out in the lives of others, especially Brian's. #doublefail). Financial failure taught me more about my life, faith, gifts—and lack thereof—than any success ever could.

Don't hear me wrong. If you've made mistakes with your money or your marriage or both, that's not a free pass to sit and wallow in your poor decisions. It doesn't mean you cash in your chips and give up the fight. And certainly you shouldn't blame others for your own choices.

However, if you have failed and then fought your way back out again, you have discovered something rather amazing. You will rarely go back to the unwise behaviors of the past. Like someone who burns herself after touching the stove, you realize it hurts to fail. It takes time and sacrifice to correct mistakes. You will do anything to avoid that pain again.

I can't tell you the number of times I've met someone who wants to get rich quick or have all the problems in their marriage vanish with a poof. Often their notions are for noble causes. After all, they just want to pay off all their debt so they can be incredibly generous. Or they want a better marriage so they can set a good example for their kids. However, when someone unexpectedly obtains money or has a harebrained scheme to fix their marriage in an instant, problems abound. Anything that prevents you from experiencing the pain of failing results in a return to borrowing money or continuing poor relationship patterns.

You've probably witnessed this truth in action before. News reports announce yet another lottery winner going completely broke. We all scratch our heads and wonder out loud, "How in the world did that happen? They had so much money!" It's really no surprise though. If you didn't walk a journey that caused sacrifice, you're highly likely to end right back on the same path you started before the "instant fix."

Why am I telling you all this? Do I want you to be a failure? Far from it. In fact my heart is for you to have a healthy, strong marriage and a healthy, strong financial future. But you have to realize that for either or both, change is required. And sometimes change can be challenging or even painful.

Paying off debt isn't complex. It's just not easy. Similarly, having an awesome marriage isn't complicated. It's just not simple.

If you've read *Slaying the Debt Dragon,* you know our plan to pay off debt wasn't an economic treatise. It wasn't highfalutin or intricate. While there were hundreds of choices (many outlined in that first book), the bottom line is that we worked many more hours and spent much less money. We took on two and then three extra jobs. We switched to a cash-based budgeting system. We planned our meals. We rarely dined out. We didn't go on vacation. We made our own laundry detergent and household cleaners. We cut any and every extra expense. We made paying off debt a game we played to win. We cut coupons. We tuned in daily to Dave Ramsey like it was an AA meeting and debt was our addiction. We budgeted, crunched the numbers, and then revisited our work to see what else we could do. We held weekly budget meetings. We communicated about even the smallest of purchases.

Our methods were simple. But I'm guessing you realize the process wasn't easy. Our story originated with a choice. Brian first cast the vision to pay off all our consumer debt. I'll admit I was skeptical. I just couldn't see how the mammoth task was possible. However, after witnessing his first steps of obedience yield results, I followed suit. I also began making simple choices to reach our complex goal. It paid off—to the tune of $127,482.30 in just under four years.

Every day you make choices. Every day you determine where your money will go and how you will treat your spouse. Every day you can choose to return to the pain and put your fingers on the stove. Or every day, you can remember, "Ouch. That hurt. Let's not do that again."

I hope you . . . embrace your failure.

Maybe it's not as poetic as a Lee Ann Womack song, but I really do hope you embrace your failure. Learn from it. Come out stronger and smarter and better equipped. Just because you've made mistakes, it doesn't mean you've been issued a toe tag or been taken out of the game.

But it does mean you have to change.

Do you want to leave a better heritage for your children? Do you want a healthier and fulfilled marriage? Do you want to be able to provide both for the needs and even some of the wants of your family? Do you want to be able to change the world?

The pain is worth the change if you are brave enough to fail.

Stop for a minute and consider the labels you've placed on your marriage. Is failure one of them? Is that such a bad thing? One thing I know for sure is that you're not the exception. You're not too far gone. There is always hope for your future.

God cares more about you than the mistakes you have made. God's love reaches beyond poor financial decisions and marital ruts. Best of all, God doesn't condemn the failure in your money or your marriage. Even if your origin story begins in failure, His loving hope is to dispel labels and rename you victorious.

The Blessed Beginning

Every great epic has an opening line and a detailed prologue.

A long time ago in a galaxy far, far away.

Two houses, both alike in dignity, in fair Verona, where we lay our scene.

It was the best of times, it was the worst of times.

In a hole in the ground, there lived a hobbit.

Your story is no different. Beginnings are blessed. Celebrate where you began.

Discussion Questions

1. Have you ever followed wrong directions? Where did you end up?
2. For Brian, the instructions of "it's the fifth house on the right" changed his path forever. What are some of the best game changer statements spoken over your life?
3. Cherie spoke of what she would say to her twenty-one-year-old self and how she would encourage twenty-two-year-old Brian. What words of wisdom would you give your beginning self at the start of your relationship with your spouse? How would you encourage your beginning spouse?
4. When have you fallen into the trap of following someone else's Dan Henrys for money or marriage? What happened as a result?

Fostering Financial Foreplay

If budget and time allow, return to the place where you and your spouse first met. You might dine at the restaurant of your first date or take a walk together in a location significant to your beginnings. If time or location constrain your efforts, take a stroll down memory lane by looking through old photos or love letters.

CHAPTER 2

What Is Financial Foreplay?

From a House Divided to a Blissful Union

Many people spend more time in planning the wedding than they do in planning the marriage.

ZIG ZIGLAR

No matter the people or places, the responses remained identical. Friend, coworker, or acquaintance: "What's the new book about?"

Us: "Financial foreplay: how smart money management habits lead to great sex in marriage."

Nine times out of ten, blank, frightened stares followed. But those same eyes flashed with enlivened interest in a matter of seconds. From our own personal experience and the hours we've shared encouraging and counseling countless other couples, we knew of the vital connection between smart finance and spicy romance. The looks exchanged from our curious counterparts confirmed we were on to something.

From this concept, we identified eight key areas where couples struggle with money and marriage—and, consequently eight areas of conflict that rarely lead to passionate encounters. No one walks down the aisle and proclaims, "I sure hope the next several decades of my life are miserable and end in deep disappointment." However, in the days, weeks, months, and years following an exchange of vows, our habits overcome naive hopes. To take our marriages from average to awesome, we must develop shared money strategies and practices.

Perfect relationships don't exist, because there are no perfect people. Two unique individuals, both made in the image of God, who both deeply love God, still struggle to merge their lives into one. *Improvement requires movement.* Regardless of the number of years you've been together or how solid or fractured your bond, fulfilling marriages arise from consistent intentional effort over time.

But back to where we began. What is financial foreplay? To us, financial foreplay simply means husbands and wives investing in smart financial habits and relational capital to clear the way for spicy sex and meaningful togetherness. It's taking care of bank business so you can get down to "business" in bed, leaving cash conflicts far behind. It's a complete trust, vulnerability, and connection when it comes to both our bodies and our budgets. Financial foreplay results from a continued mutual pursuit of improved shared money habits and communication. As couples become more adept at navigating the difficult waters of finances, they develop a transferable skill set. The ability to communicate clearly, remain organized, focus on shared priorities, handle conflict, and lead together well, removes barriers to a deeper and more intimate connection, allowing more room and desire for sex. The closer you move toward one another in your finances, the closer you feel, and the more you anticipate growing together emotionally and physically.

Managing money together is tough. In a recent study, researchers determined that 70 percent of couples fought more about money than "household chores, togetherness, sex, snoring, and what's for dinner."[1] If you fight about money once or more a week, your odds of getting a divorce go up by 30 percent.[2] According to a 2012 study, frequent financial arguments are far and away the greatest predictor of divorce.[3]

We designed *Your Money, Your Marriage* to help you beat those odds. If arguments about money pull you apart, then agreements about money can't help but push you together. Each chapter tackles a sticky marital situation and describes a movement from old patterns of enslaving behavior to new unifying freedoms. We'll begin with an exploration of true intimacy, the need for security, and how to connect on a deeper level.

Let the financial foreplay begin.

Cargo Cult: Brian

During World War II, Japanese forces occupied tiny undeveloped Pacific islands. Inhabitants watched in reverent awe as cargo planes regularly landed and unloaded food, supplies, and munitions. Toward the end of the war, American soldiers advanced and replaced the opposing Japanese soldiers. Planes still whooshed in and out of the islands. The people, flags, and ideologies changed, but those facts went unnoticed by the natives.

After the war, the planes stopped landing. With no use for strategic supply stations, Americans pulled out of the Pacific islands. WWII ended, and in the eyes of an industrialized world, nothing on the islands merited rebuilding. The people who lived on these islands, however, hatched a plan to entice the planes to return, despite their lack of any modern technology.

The indigenous people replicated large satellite-dish-shaped "radar" receptors out of natural earthen materials like matted grasses, sticks, and leaves. But the cargo planes never landed. They thrashed a makeshift runway through overgrown foliage and lit torches down either side. But the cargo planes never landed. They fashioned and wore hand-carved headsets with bamboo antennae. But the cargo planes never landed again. With painstaking detail, the aboriginals recreated everything they saw and mimicked the movements of the Japanese and American troops. Perhaps most impressive, they sculpted full-scale model planes from island materials in the hope of attracting real cargo planes. But of course, the cargo planes never landed.

Because of the religious fervor with which the natives tried to conjure deities (cargo planes) from the sky, scientists labeled the phenomenon as a cargo cult. A quick internet search reveals images of the cargo cult's handiwork. Our twenty-first-century, first-world eyes recognize these amusing rudimentary creations were destined for failure. Trying to lure and land a plane with a hand-carved headset is absurd. So why do we all wear bamboo antennae in our marriages?

Just like the cargo cults had unattainable expectations, we

shoulder unrealistic expectations about money and intimacy in our marriages. In an effort to grow closer together, we take fancy vacations and buy expensive gifts. Maybe it's a diamond tennis bracelet or a Rolex watch instead of bamboo antennae, but the result is the same: our expectations go unmet. We resemble a cargo cult when we keep using the same methodologies to build intimacy when those habits continue to fail. What's worse than the cargo cult example is that our expensive gestures to each other actually cause dissension. The gestures fall flat and our bank accounts dwindle, so we fight about money. The cycle damages our relationships, but we don't learn from the experience. Instead, we repeat the whole destructive pattern over and over again. We're inadvertently building a cargo cult while tearing down our marriages.

For example, anytime we model a fictional marriage, we're building a cargo cult marriage. If our idealized version of sex and romance stems from a reality dating show, we're trending toward cargo cult status. Those shows exist for ratings and portray warped versions of love. Copying the dialogue and actions we see on-screen invites disappointment. Handing your spouse a rose is nice, but it doesn't enhance real intimacy. The more we desire our marriages to resemble television relationships, the less likely a plane carrying real intimacy will land.

Less obvious cargo cult participation occurs when we imitate selective conduct of other healthy relationships. Having couples in our lives who are more experienced and possess financial wisdom and marital intimacy helps us grow. But if one of those couples goes on a Mediterranean cruise, it doesn't mean you go on a cruise too. The cruise happened as a result of a lifetime of intimacy and financial security; it doesn't necessarily build either one. Learn from mentors, but don't mimic everything people in healthy marriages do; mirror who they are. Their daily money habits and tender moments are more important than the flashy and admittedly appealing events. Choosing to replicate the vacation instead of daily growth will not land a plane full of intimacy.

Just as the cargo cults of the Pacific islands were missing technological advancements, our counterfeit efforts for intimacy are missing sacrificial love and commitment. Without sacrificial love and commitment, we're just fidgeting around with gestures resembling intimacy but absent of depth.

An actual commitment to your finances develops intimacy. Money and security are inextricably linked. Financial commitment emulates God's sacrificial love for us. His love tells us "I'm going to do whatever it takes to care for you. You are more important than anything." And even when we recognize on a soul-level that God is our only source of security, taking care of our finances sends that same message to our spouse: "I'm going to do whatever it takes to care for you. You are more important than anything." Every time you tend to your finances, you tend to your spouse. Frequent moments of financial fidelity increase the security and trust you have in one another. That security brings you from separate individuals to a bonded couple.

Two becoming one in marriage is more than just sex. Granted, sex in marriage is the ultimate symbol of love and oneness. But having sex without intimacy is no different than wearing a bamboo headset and expecting a plane to land. You are going through the motions, but there is no real connection. Connection makes a successful marriage and leads to financial foreplay.

Bamboo headsets don't work because they are imitations. We can avoid cargo cult marriage by revisiting our commitments to one another. Unlike bamboo headsets, these commitments are real. Keeping shared promises nurtures true intimacy.

Money Vows: Cherie

Most of my life, I've lived a girl-power narrative. My childhood heroes were always strong, smart women: Wonder Woman, Scarlett from G.I. Joe, Princess Leia, and my mom (awwww, but true). Spinning around in circles in my backyard, I would imagine my play clothes transforming into the red and blue hues of superhero armor. My trusty lasso at my side, I imitated Lynda Carter's smooth moves by tossing tennis balls to touch the surface of the moon, or maybe just the top of our ranch home until they bounced down the other side.

My childhood ambitions reached beyond saving the world though. Days filled with playing the heroine were accompanied by imagining my potential future. More than once, I donned a white pillowcase while clutching an invisible bouquet, walking down a make-believe aisle. I dreamed of my wedding day, planning the colors of the napkins (why this was so important in the 80s and 90s, I'll never understand), the variety of flowers, and, of course, the face of my handsome groom.

What I never considered, though, were the words we'd speak to one another when I met the man of my dreams at the front of the church. I assumed you just went with whatever the preacher suggested—the "to have and to hold, for richer or for poorer, in sickness and in health" bit. Honestly, who really cared about those words anyway? In my childhood fantasies, the climactic moment was when my mystery man pulled the veil back, revealing my shining face, and we shared a long, sweet symbolic kiss (a gesture which as a kid always seemed kind of gross and compelling at the same time).

Brian and I have lost count of the number of weddings we've attended over the last two decades. Some that flutter to the top of our list were touching weddings filled with significance and centered on

Jesus. At the best receptions we danced until our feet ached. There were weddings where it seemed like we knew everyone in attendance and others where we looked around longing for a friendly face beyond the bride and the groom. We've encountered our fair share of odd DJs too—including one guy who quipped that the newly wedded couple was headed to the Virgin Islands that night but that they wouldn't be the Virgin Islands for long (wrong, just wrong).

We love weddings. Each time a couple takes steps toward each other (especially when those steps are taken toward following Jesus closer too), we feel a renewal of the bond we experienced on July 17, 1999. Hearing others repeat the same vows we did strengthens the connection we share. As different and unique as every wedding has been, almost every ceremony we've attended shares a similar ritual. Whether the newlyweds light candles, combine sand in a jar, braid cords together, or assemble a cross, each service climaxes with an illustrative gesture.

The metaphorical action represents a greater truth of two lives joining as one. If only joining finances could be as easy. Wouldn't that be lovely? We both pour a little glass of sand into a bigger jar and—*boom*—we agree on every money decision. Or we mingle the flame of two candles into one larger wick and henceforth we never have another financial disagreement again. No matter how fairytale-like the wedding, no marriage fits this unrealistic notion.

As children we may dream of our splendid future weddings, but rarely do we think of promises made at the end of the aisle. Even as grown-up engaged couples, it's easier to get caught up in the traditions and symbols—the rings, the centerpieces, the cake, the clothes—forgetting the solemn vows we are about to make. We zero in on the details, skipping over the key component of any wedding ceremony.

Whether we repeat a time-honored script or write words of our own, the vows we speak are what really make a wedding a wedding. Again, the symbols are beautiful examples of our intentions to lead a life intertwined, but the words we speak out loud travel into the real stuff of marriage beyond simple symbolism. Lighting a candle is lovely but vowing to remain with your husband or wife whether you are richer or poorer packs a punch. Promising a lifetime of caring for your spouse in times of sickness and in health carries more weight than combining sand. You are giving your word before God, family, and friends to remain true to each other no matter what curveballs life may throw your way.

Over the years, as we've coached couples beginning their new lives together or those who have been thrown off course by one of those aforementioned curveballs, I've longed for an expanded version of wedding vows. Even in our own marital struggles, I've wished we would have made more spelled-out promises, especially when it comes to money. So one day Brian and I drafted what we call money vows—promises we've made to one another, reaching beyond symbols and into the most intimate parts of life.

I promise to . . .

- share freely the money I make, resisting the temptation to see what's mine as mine and what's yours as yours.
- never lie or avoid talking about what I've spent.
- refrain from hiding or hoarding money.
- never make a major purchase without consulting you first.
- relinquish notions of what I think is best and focus on what we both agree on.
- be faithful, not only in our sex lives, but also to the agreements we've made together about our finances.

- recognize that everything we have belongs to God, and He's called us to manage our family, time, resources, possessions, and finances together.

Promises made and kept provide security in marriage. Security results in intimacy. Only when we feel safe do we feel completely open and vulnerable. No one wants to get naked with someone they can't trust. And while your wife may not immediately take your hand and lead you to the bedroom after you make these promises, she is more likely to feel comfortable with you when you prove true to your word.

Financial infidelity, much like sexual infidelity, breaks the bond of trust and security between husbands and wives. Once broken, that space of vulnerability and nakedness is difficult to recreate. Your money vows can look like ours or take a form of their own. But whatever you and your spouse agree on, keep your word. Make promises out loud that move beyond symbolism. Remain true.

Everyone Needs Rumble Strips: Brian

Honnnnkkk! The car's horn blared its unpleasant tone. My eyes flashed open, and my teenage hands jerked the steering wheel to the left, forcing my car back onto the roadway, narrowly missing a telephone pole. Long denying my body's need for rest, I fell asleep at the wheel in the middle of a sunny Tuesday. As it turns out, cars are difficult to drive when you're asleep, and mine substituted someone's large front yard for a public thoroughfare. Fortunately, the conscientious driver behind me blasted the best warning device he had to wake me from my afternoon slumber.

If we fall asleep at the wheel in our cars, we risk extraordinary damage. When we fall asleep at the wheel of our money or our marriage, we jeopardize our sacred bonds. Every marriage is susceptible to drifting outside the lanes, wrecking finances and relationships. Maybe someone will relentlessly honk a horn and alert you; but we can't always rely on that. We can employ, however, a device highway contractors designed to save the lives of drowsy drivers.

On most modern interstates, a path of corrugated pavement lines the edge of both the far left and far right lanes. If your car drifts outside its designated lane, the tires and the uneven surface combine for a vicious vibration and an irritating buzzing noise. While I'm sure a more official name exists, the common term for this roughened pavement is a "rumble strip."

Connectedness is our goal in money and in marriage. Installing rumble strips in our lives helps us avoid misery and connects us in a blissful union. If you have agreed to a budget with your spouse, the budget itself serves as a pretty good rumble strip. Let's say you receive an email from your favorite shoe store notifying you of steep clearance markdowns. If you do not have a line item for antique burgundy Johnston & Murphy bicycle toe lace-up oxfords in your budget, there's a sound you should hear in your head: *rumble rumble*. Spending off budget breaches trust. Even if Johnston & Murphy miraculously starts manufacturing cordovan shoes for the adult male, shoe miracles don't justify budget blunders.

Thinking about buying new furniture without your spouse's input? *Rumble rumble*. Taking an "ask for forgiveness later" approach and buying the kids a puppy against your spouse's wishes? *Rumble rumble*. Filling out a credit card application to "save" 10 percent? *Rumble* stinkin' *rumble*. These should all be relatively easy responses, but the practice of hearing the rumble noise in your head (or making it out loud) will help you turn your life's wheel back toward where it needs to be. Don't fall asleep at the wheel of your finances. Even more so, stay awake at matters of the heart.

If you want to crush your spouse and pulverize her heart into dust, have an affair with someone. Nothing diminishes an intimate connection between married couples more. Affairs do not typically begin with, "Hi, my name is Steve. It's a pleasure to meet you. Would you like to have sex and destroy our respective families?" Infidelity culminates from several choices over a long period of time that rumble strips could have prevented. For example, fellas, if a female coworker asks you for a ride home, *rumble rumble*. If a high school girlfriend sends you a social media friend request out of the blue, *rumble rumble*. If either spouse refers to another member of the opposite sex as their "best friend," *rumble rumble*.

Ultimately, you both need to work together to establish rumble strips with your money vows and your marriage vows. Remember, rumble strips on the highway are very close to the outside lanes and warn you at the first sign of drifting. The rumble strips in your lives need to be as close to the straight and narrow as possible.

Making Space in Your Budget for Romance: Cherie

Early in our marriage, I sat nervously sweating in a room of women similar in age and stage of life. We read a book together and had some frank conversations about the realities of marriage and sex. Overall, it had been an eye-opening experience for me and was one of the first times other women shared their intimate struggles in a healthy and God-honoring manner. But this particular week a guest speaker came in to share some of the specific ways she and her husband placed a priority on romance. From ending each and *every* evening sharing a bowl of ice cream in the tub (I'm still not sure we're coordinated enough to pull this one off. Maybe our tub is just too small?) to candlelight dinners prepared from ALDI (much more my speed), this couple learned to keep love alive without dropping too much cash.

I love a good bargain, so this advice made sense to me. That was until she began talking about buying lingerie from secondhand stores. I shuddered at the thought of wearing someone else's underwear, even if it had been washed in my home. Look, this frugal girl has her limits. I'm sure I do plenty of things that might gross out the wise woman who just wanted to help me have a better marriage. But I couldn't hear another word after she mentioned her sexy money-saving hack. Nope.

Kudos to you if you can scare up a great slinky at the thrift store. Cognitively, I know washing the item makes it "like new," but I can't get over the icky mental hump. But this teachable moment did help me realize a number of life lessons. (1) This strategy would definitely not work if you have a husband with germophobe tendencies. Say, a guy who barely touches doorknobs. Let's just say I know someone. (2) When it comes to lingerie, frills can be fun, though many fellas also appreciate the color naked. (3) It's important to budget for romance, even if you're living on limited resources.

While we were paying off $127,000 in debt, we devoted each and every extra penny we earned to our financial goals. We didn't have enough money to pay a babysitter, let alone enjoy a fancy dinner out on the town. Honestly, there weren't even funds for secondhand negligees (thank goodness for teachable moment lesson number two). We even paused from giving each other gifts for Christmas, birthdays, anniversaries, Valentine's Day, and "just because." There were no romantic weekends away to exotic destinations or couples-only trips. But we derived just as much pleasure from working together toward a common financial goal as any purchased present.

Somehow we still managed to scrape up enough money for an occasional moment together. It honestly wasn't about how much we spent. Instead, setting aside money—no matter how small the amount—made us realize that romance is a priority in our marriage. Don't misunderstand me. Love and sex don't depend on spending money. You can have both in spades without cracking open your piggy bank. However, placing a value on romance by setting aside hard-earned cash with the intention of investing in the flourishing of your love speaks volumes about the importance you place on the intimate bonds of your marriage.

Use the money you set aside however you both see fit. You could spend your romance budget on one nice evening out per month. Or you could roll over the dollar amount until you save up enough for a weekend getaway. Even if you only have a dollar apiece, you can go to the dollar store to purchase special gifts for each other. Your spending doesn't have to be flashy. You could even use your romance budget to purchase secondhand lingerie. I promise I won't even judge. Just don't tell me, okay?

Whatever you choose to do, place a priority on spending money in a way that develops your love for one another and enhances your intimacy. Already feeling stretched financially and not sure where your romance budget might come from? Check out these ideas to kick-start your funds:

- **Save your change.** Each time you receive a dime, penny, quarter, or nickel, place that change into a jar. Once you fill up the jar or reach a specific date, count the money and plan to invest in romance.
- **Sell some stuff.** Books, exercise equipment, home decor, outgrown toys and clothes, household goods you never

use . . . your junk might be someone else's treasure. Hold an online yard sale to begin building your love fund.

- **Set a percentage.** Each month, set a small percentage (it could even be as little as 1 percent) to save toward your marriage enrichment fund. When your income arrives in your checking account, calculate that percentage and withdraw the set amount. Place it in a savings account or even in your change jar. An automated version of this practice works even better.
- **Specify a goal.** Saving without a specific end in mind can become burdensome and feel pointless. Whether you choose a marriage conference, a beach getaway, or simply a new restaurant you'd like to try together, set an explicit goal for your romance budget. Do research on where you'd like to go, and, if possible, set a date on the calendar. Clear-cut plans yield concrete results.

Beating the Odds

Here's what we'd love more than anything else after you finish reading this book—for you to be free of financial anxiety and have awesome intimacy with your spouse. A financially healthy marriage leads you toward a steamy sex life—we fully believe that. The trust and vulnerability you share when it comes to money transfers to the bedroom. Financial foreplay is a glorious and exciting state of being and is one you can obtain.

It's unfair of us to make this kind of promise without supplying you with the tools necessary to accomplish such lofty goals. As we mentioned in the introduction, at the close of each chapter, you'll find not only questions to guide your conversations, but also activities to foster financial foreplay. Hopefully you've already completed the exercises at the close of chapter one.

We want to reemphasize the importance of these helpful practices. We can't force you to work through the material. But we promise, if you just let your marriage happen, it will fail. In order for your relationship to improve, you must move from a house divided to a more blissful union. Doing that requires some legwork and action on your part.

The odds and conventional thinking pile up against you. Those odds, however, are not insurmountable. Don't let the failure of others define your financial or marital future. Your money and your marriage are destined for great things. Positive, intentional, coordinated effort always defies statistics. You can do it.

Strive toward authentic intimacy. Be faithful to your vows. Make wise choices to keep your relationship on the road.

Investing in your romance by applying these concepts opens the door to financial foreplay. Who wouldn't want more of that?

Discussion Questions

1. What's the best wedding you've ever attended? What's the weirdest wedding you've ever attended?
2. Have you ever known someone who used the wrong methodology to gain marital intimacy (akin to wearing a bamboo headset)?
3. Did you write your own marriage vows? Which promises that you made became more "real" to

you after you'd been married awhile? Handwrite or type your original wedding vows. Post them on your refrigerator or bathroom mirror to remind yourself of the promises you've made.

4. Have you ever accidentally driven off the road? What happened?
5. What are some rumble strips—safeguards to protect your relationships—that you have in your marriage or personal life? What are some rumble strips that would be beneficial to employ?
6. Do you currently have a marriage investment fund? If you don't, how could you start one? How would you spend the dollars you save?

Fostering Financial Foreplay

- Together with your spouse, compose your own money vows. Speak them out loud to each other. Remain true to the promises you make. Renew your vows as necessary.
- Target a dollar amount that you will set aside as a part of your romance budget. Choose one of the methods Cherie mentions to begin building a fund meant only for activities to enhance romance and build intimacy in your marriage.

CHAPTER 3

What Did You Say?

From Different Books to the Same Page

Huh?

EVERY SPOUSE EVER FROM THE OTHER ROOM

In theory, the process of communication is simple. You speak, your spouse hears. Your spouse speaks, you hear. You nod your heads robotically in agreement, and as in a picture-perfect world or a *Stepford Wives*-style 1950s movie, you gleefully hold hands and skip down the sunshiny lane together. Roll credits.

However, we've never seen communication in our own marriage play out this way. Real communication between a husband and a wife on any issue—from choosing new carpet to planning the weekend—walks boldly into tension. Given our unique upbringings, our varying God-given gifts, and our past relationships, we embody a wide range of opinions, values, and dreams. Melding those soul marking experiences into one unified front is a wee bit more complicated than holding hands and skipping down the road.

In marriage, we come to each other beautifully broken, both marred and magnificent from the lives we lived before we said, "I do." Thinking we could instantaneously become one in thought, soul, and opinion deceives us into an unrealistic view of communication. And yet somehow we need to find acceptable and effective strategies to communicate about everything in our shared lives—from who will be where when tomorrow to what our marriage will look like in thirty, forty, fifty, or sixty years, and beyond.

Explicit communication reigns supreme when it comes to sex and money. Without knowing our partner's wants, desires, expectations, and dreams, we fall into a pit of assumptions and accusations. Without clearly expressing our own wants, desires, expectations, and dreams, we tumble into disappointment and despair.

Thankfully, we've witnessed some couples nail the practice of explicit communication. Together, they charted a path toward paying off debt and achieved their goals. Their regular respectful discussions about spending and trimming household expenses for a greater common purpose yielded success. Unfortunately, we've also observed unhealthy financial communication between husbands and wives. Secret purchases, grudge holding, and unfair accusations caused their relationships to crumble. Phrases like the following rarely result in greater intimacy:

- You bought *another* pair of shoes?
- You wanna do it?

- It's my money and I'll spend it however I want.
- I forgot to tell you that I went ahead and bought the newest iPhone.
- You always . . .
- You never . . .
- Shouldn't you always be in the mood to have sex?

Around half of all couples keep separate financial accounts.[1] One in three married people have lied to their spouse about money.[2] By definition, lying ranks as ineffective communication. Separating our finances and choosing poor communication (or none at all) leads us to disconnect in our sex lives too. We compartmentalize what's yours and mine until metaphorically we're sleeping in our own twin beds like Cherie's grandparents Hubert and Beulah did. We're sure it was just because of their bad backs, but it still seems pretty weird.

The most searched combination of words regarding marriage is "sexless marriage." Over twenty-one thousand Google users per month type those words into the one place most people are bold enough to be honest: the search bar.[3] These searches outpace the next-best contender, "unhappy marriage," threefold. Couples aren't talking to each other about their struggles with sex and money. But what if they did?

Effective communication doesn't just help you get on the same page financially. Effective communication moves you into the same bed sexually.

Worth the Wait: Brian

Before Cherie came down the aisle to meet me at the altar, circumstance placed me isolated in a windowless cinderblock choir room of the church where we were soon to be married. After what felt like hours, the pastor of the church joined me and led me to my spot at the front of the sanctuary. The wait was worth it. Captivated by her beauty and entranced by the notion of our impending future, my heart pounded in anticipation. After waiting hours alone in a church cage, I was still willing to wait as long as it took for Cherie to walk to me. This was our day. She was my bride. I would have waited for her until the end of time.

In spite of the rapturous anticipation, grooms are patient. No groom stands at the altar during his bride's processional and hollers, "Hurry up, we don't have all day!" Brides are similar in their patience. No bride sprints down the aisle like The Ultimate Warrior to the ring and shouts, "Let's get this over with!" The anticipation of a wedding ceremony is exhilarating. The anticipation makes the wait worthwhile.

Anticipation is a powerful and rewarding experience. The best part about Christmas morning for a kid is the anticipation. An entire online subculture is devoted to the unboxing of items. You can find over six-and-a-half *years* worth of videos on YouTube, with people fraught with anticipation to open everything from tech to toys.[4] When you await and look forward to an event on your calendar, the anticipation creates much of the memory associated with the event. In the marital relationship, the anticipation and allure of sex makes it all the more appealing, fulfilling, and memorable. Anticipation can be the best part of sex.

Over time we lose the sense of anticipation that we savored on our wedding day. Restoring that same spirit of suspense adds excitement for your shared financial dreams and draws you closer together fiscally and physically. Consider a wedding ceremony. The event's success depends on clearly communicated and understood expectations. Bride walks to groom. The odds of her running out of the building are surprisingly low. A crowd of people stands in delight when she enters the room and all eyes are on her. She paces to the front, a member of the clergy reads from a predetermined script, and both bride and groom leave together. The wedding party also practiced the entire ceremony at something called a rehearsal.

At a rehearsal, the future couple discusses and walks through what's going to happen at the main event. Nobody likes surprises on their wedding day. Anticipation flips to anxiety in a New York minute when unexpected variables enter the equation. Much in the same way a rehearsal and clear communication about the wedding ceremony helps build anticipation of a new shared life together, clear communication leads to marked improvements and anticipation in every aspect of married life. As married couples, we benefit from taking time to plan and discuss what we want our future with each other to look like. How much more should we employ the strategies of our wedding rehearsal to our marriage—the true main event? When you begin to plan your goals together, you create anticipation and amplify excitement together as you move toward each goal. Communication enhances anticipation. In essence, anticipation is foreplay. Because of its critical role, we must ensure we're communicating with each other well.

Marriages rise and fall on the quality of their communication. Be grace-filled with your spouse and know it takes time and practice to improve. Successful communication also hinges on the humility to admit you're wrong, the courage to say you don't know, and the honesty to acknowledge when you don't understand what the other person told you. When you leverage effective communication, you and your spouse will vanquish any obstacle in your way.

At some point after the wedding ceremony, the patient groom, who would have waited an eternity for his bride, leaves his patient ways behind. The bride exchanges her slow, deliberate pace for the hurried hustle and bustle of everyday life, the thrill of anticipation forgotten.

Practiced and frequent communication resurrects the same heart-pounding, awestruck anticipation of your wedding day. What if we conduct our marriages like the wedding processional never stopped? What if we returned to a time when our hearts thundered with anticipation at the thought of our future together? That harmonious future with our spouse still lies ahead. The processional is a continuum. Just as you were patient on your wedding day, be patient now. He is worth the wait. She is worth the wait.

It may seem like you've been waiting forever to get on the same page about money. Financial communication skills don't develop overnight, but they are well within your reach and are worth the wait. Anticipating a unified vision for your money and your marriage should drive you wild with expectation.

Playing Charades: Cherie

As a kid I thought my dad had the weirdest, best job in the world. During the late 70s and 80s, he worked in technology for a company that compiled the "let your fingers do the walking" book. You've heard of it—that ancient artifact known as the phonebook, also used as a doorstop. On the rare occasion we receive one now, it goes straight into the recycling bin. Dad spent his days in a giant room filled with seven-foot machines winding data around enormous spools of tape. The noise was so loud that I'm surprised he can still hear after decades of exposure to the high decibels.

His work also involved fixing machines whenever they crashed.

Because my mom didn't want to be alone with a young family in rural Indiana, often our entire family went with Dad to his office in the middle of the night. I can remember running around the workspace, tracing the cubicle walls with my finger, and building up enough of an electric charge to shock the holy snot out of my brother when he came at me from around the corner. I also remember snooping in the other employees' desk drawers (who were not on call like my dad) and removing all their paper clips so I could make a shiny chain necklace. If that weren't awesome enough, my brother and I greedily snatched up all their rubber bands so we could have an all-out war, ducking in and out from under desks and snapping the long, stringy, brown office supplies at each other (ouch).

But the very best office supplies at my dad's job were larger-than-life sketch pads. Used for planning and brainstorming at work, items like these were rare in homes. Remember, there weren't office supply chains, and the big-box retailer was just coming into being in our small hometown. When there was a sheet or two left on a pad, Dad was allowed to bring these amazing, huge blank slates home to our family. On family game nights, we gathered around a stand he built to stabilize the oversized notebook and played the classic 1980s board game Win, Lose, or Draw, using pungent black markers.

Similar to Pictionary or one of our girls' favorite board games, Who, What, Where (you should totally play it!), Win, Lose, or Draw is the artistic equivalent to charades. Without talking, one player attempts to sketch a particular topic on paper, while their team frantically guesses the answer before the timer dings. Hilarity ensues as those of us who are less than artistically inclined crudely sketch out our best stick figures, leaving everyone in the audience confused and at a loss.

Communication in marriage can feel like a brutal game of Win,

Lose, or Draw. One spouse attempts to guess what the other is trying to say. We feel embarrassed at the difficulty and our inability to both convey and receive the message. Oftentimes, we start all over again but employ the exact same methods by drawing the exact same picture while circling and pointing at it with frustration, mystified why the other party can't guess what we're trying to draw. We groan, roll our eyes, and turn back to the drawing board, adding a new detail to the picture. The process exhausts us, and with no timer to bring the game to an end, the cycle repeats over and over again.

A marriage marked by financial foreplay requires us to learn how to be verbal in a world that's increasingly becoming more and more nonverbal. These days, I talk on the phone to only three people: my mom, Brian, and my friend Tricia. Even my texts have become less verbal. I use emojis and GIFs to convey what probably could be paragraphs of words. Don't get me wrong. Texting is a great tool when you're married. It helps you determine who's picking up the kids and what you're eating for dinner. Texting allows us to relay sweet messages of love in the middle of a mundane day or ask an important, quick question. However, texting is not talking. And if we long to be on the same page financially, we have to learn to talk to one another using real words, face-to-face, not winky-eyed smileys left open to interpretation.

But don't think you can just get away with speaking in a robotic voice. Your context and tone are just as important as the words spoken. Did you know that 85 percent of even face-to-face communication is nonverbal?[5] From the way you position your body, to the movement of your eyes, to the sound of your voice when you speak, you're saying much more than you think you are. In fact, I've learned the difficult way that *how you say something matters more than what you actually say.*

Take for instance the words *I'm sorry*. Said in a sincere tone, this phrase expresses remorse and regret, maybe even the potential for repentance or a change in behavior. However, when forced to be spoken between our two daughters who have injured each other in an act of tomfoolery, they come across with an entirely different meaning. Gritted teeth, crossed arms, and mumbled dialect suggest the words are less than sincere and filled with zero remorse or regret. Of course, our kids are perfect and would never talk to one another like this or land in a situation requiring us as parents to inflict such a punishment. It's all hypothetical. Also, note how the tone of my words (ahem, sarcastic) changes the entire meaning of the last two sentences.

Author Truman Capote penned the words, "The quietness of his tone italicized the malice of his reply."[6] Your tone of voice transforms the words you use faster than using all caps on a tweet or status update. Don't underestimate the power of the sound of your speech in the context of communication within your marriage.

In the same fashion, receiving the words of your spouse can be equally important. A wise philosopher (or an internet meme) I once read said it's important to "Listen with your eyes." The words turned over in my mind for days, and I began to question whether or not I listen with my eyes when Brian speaks to me. I know that some (but not all) of the time, I do. I also know that some (but not all) of the time, I do not. I recognized this once when Brian kindly suggested he'd like to remove my phone from my hands and wing it on the street in front of our house if I did not look up and acknowledge him speaking to me. Whoops.

Let's be fully active when our spouses are trying to speak. No heads buried in devices, no attention turned to whatever you were doing before he or she entered the room. Our body language, attentiveness, and active listening determine future conversations. From firsthand experience, I know full well this is not an easy task. Our conversations in the kitchen are often punctuated with timers on the stove buzzing, children asking for homework help, music in the background, things falling, and once (ok, maybe twice) things catching on fire. Hey, I'm no Julia Child. It's a challenge in the real world. For this reason, when Brian and I attempt to have a serious conversation, we try to reserve those moments of communication for times of minimal distraction.

Ideally, any conversations about money and/or budgeting occur after our daughters have gone to bed. We power down our devices, place them in another room, and face one another. Sometimes we place our hands palms up—a physical gesture indicating our openness toward one another and the attempt to let go of selfish desires. These small physical acts prepare our hearts, souls, minds, and bodies to authentically engage with one another.

The more we communicate with our bodies and our words about our finances, the more open we both are when it comes to sex too. It's tempting to separate these distinct areas of our marriage, relegating our money to one file folder in the cabinet of our marriage and intimacy to another. However, on occasion when we've gone to bed after spatting about money because we've not practiced smart communication (alas, we let the sun go down on our anger), we've found ourselves clinging to our respective edges of the bed. We placed as much physical space between us as possible, reflecting the immense, rugged gap between our hearts. Maybe you've experienced this too?

Look, I get it. Communication and marriage aren't nearly as simple as a game of Win, Lose, or Draw. You don't get to add a mark to your "team" score on the oversized notepad with each successful conversation. And sometimes, no one wins. But the battle of learning to convey and receive messages, over time, builds positive results within your money and your marriage. What once felt awkward and frustrating becomes more natural and productive. Even after decades, you may still have your clumsy and hilarious moments when it comes to talking about both sex and money. Don't give up hope. Again, financial foreplay takes time, practice, humility, and most of all patience.

Seven Things to Say to Your Spouse to Improve Your Money and Your Marriage

Fostering financial foreplay isn't for wimps. Communication is key. These seven intentional phrases will improve your money and your marriage each time you speak them.

1. It's going to be okay.

Sometimes handling money feels scary! Some of us flip out and fear the worst—that we will lose our homes, our health, our marriages, and more. You need to reassure your spouse that *it will be okay.* No matter what obstacles you face, or how bruised and bumped your heart might feel, there is always hope. Help your spouse avoid freak-out mode by repeating these five simple words.

2. I love you.

Travel back in time (use the Scooby-Doo sound effects if you need to). Remember walking down the aisle? How your heart was aflutter with such strong emotions? Remember saying "I do"? Financial foreplay requires returning to a place of overwhelming love and adoration. It's easiest to blame the people we are closest to for all our problems. And it's especially difficult to say "I love you" when they may have actually contributed to those problems. We all own part of our money predicaments. Don't shut down your heart. Remember that you chose your spouse and they chose you. Return to your vows. Say "I love you" frequently and sincerely.

3. You matter more.

It's tempting to get caught up in the pursuit of paying off debt or saving for the future and lose sight of why you're doing what you're doing. The temptation amplifies within a marital relationship. Pause and take time to tell your spouse they matter more than any money goal. While becoming financially sound is a noble pursuit, you still want to be married at the end of the journey. People are always more important than things. People—especially husbands and wives—take priority.

4. How are you?

You need to routinely check in on the emotional status of your husband or wife. Great financial endeavors are emotionally grueling. While we were paying off our debt, we both swung wide pendulums of emotions (we had *all* the feelings!). Check in on your spouse and ask this simple question. You may have no idea of his or her current status.

5. Thank you.

Appreciating your spouse's contributions to your household finances breathes life into your marriage. Maybe he works long hours. Maybe she spends more time with the kids all by herself because of those long hours. Maybe she cuts costs in every area of the budget. Maybe you both sacrifice recreational time. Affirm each other's sacrifices to improve your money and your marriage. Be sure to pause, look your spouse in the eyes, and say thank you.

6. What can I do to help?

Author and pastor Andy Stanley posits this is the most powerful question in the universe. We believe this one question could save your marriage. Asking "What can I do to help?" gives your spouse room to breathe and demonstrates your willingness to leverage your gifts and abilities to further their personal pursuits. If your spouse responds to the question, be sure to follow through.

7. Let's dream big.

Dreaming big captivates our hearts. Over the years, questions like "What would we do with our money if we weren't sinking so much of it into payments, interest, and debt?" lit us up. Dreaming big allows us to envision a future for our family, community, and world, where we can do fun things, be generous, and make a difference. Where would you go? How would your children's future look different? How could you transform your community or even the world? Dream big.

All We Need Is a Little Patience: Brian

When the young woman approached me after a church service with tears welled up in her eyes, I didn't know what to say. Cherie and I had just finished speaking to a large congregation and greeted people at a book signing after the service. We shared our story of paying off debt and how God worked in our hearts more than in our finances. The tearful young woman picked up on something she felt disqualified her from a life of financial freedom. Cherie and I worked together. Holding back a full-on cry, she confessed she and her husband were not on the same page with their faith or their finances. Sadly, I lacked adequate answers and the requisite time to field her query. So I punted. A khaki-panted church elder caught my eye, and I ushered the spirit-crushed woman to him for restoration and wise, ongoing counsel. My failure to respond never sat well with me. What troubles me more are the countless similar inquiries we have received over the last few years.

Whether it's through social media or at speaking events, the most common and most difficult-to-answer question we receive resembles some version of: "How do I get my spouse on the same page about money?" For years I prayed for a pithy, sagacious retort. I prayed I wouldn't leave another sobbing and broken soul hanging again. Fortunately, God, as He always does, had the answer waiting for me all along.

> There's more to come: We continue to shout our praise even when we're hemmed in with troubles, because we know how troubles can develop *passionate patience* in us, and how that patience in turn forges the tempered steel of virtue, keeping us alert for whatever God will do next. In alert expectancy such as this, we're never left feeling shortchanged. Quite the contrary—we can't round up enough containers to hold everything God generously pours into our lives through the Holy Spirit!
>
> **ROMANS 5:3–5 MSG (EMPHASIS MINE)**

That phrase, *passionate patience*, leapt from the page even though I'd read the passage before. The starting point for resolving troubles, including money and marriage problems, begins with passionate patience. We are *always* surrounded with troubles in this world. We often feel hemmed in, trapped, and hopeless, especially regarding our finances. Your troubled feelings compound when it seems your spouse remains on a different financial page.

You're the saver; she's the spender.

You're the long-term planner; he's the short-term, day-to-day guy.

You both feel shortchanged, like you are doing this money thing by yourself.

You might mistake the "trouble" referred to in this passage as your spouse. However, the financial strain or lack of margin in your lives is the trouble, *not* your husband or wife.

How to Develop Passionate Patience

Passionate patience forges the tempered steel of virtue.

I love that phrase in *The Message* because, fun fact: beyond being one of the strongest building materials, steel stretches farther than Gumby on muscle relaxers. Steel is actually more elastic than rubber. Through passionate patience, each of us grows—stretching like steel—in strength and character. Strength of character keeps you alert to the imminent unveiling of God's plan for your life. This alert expectancy, rooted in God's unwavering faithfulness, both excites us and compels us to action. Invariably, passionate patience yields contentment. Romans 5 is God's gentle admonition against being consumed by possessions and the treasures of this earth because we are already lavished upon with the gifts of the Holy Spirit. We can't even contain all that God has given us, and worldly goods pale in comparison to divine gifts.

Passionate patience entails an active waiting. Passion and patience originate from the same root word—a verb which means "suffering." The connotation that waiting for our spouse requires suffering is not pleasant or popular in our comfort-based culture. However, possessing a continual willingness to sacrifice for your husband or wife inspires a heart-change toward money in your spouse. Ultimately, *your* heart and *your* behavior must change before your spouse's transformation begins. Your grand or even solemn acts of financial prudence and offering of yourself will also not go unnoticed by God.

Developing passionate patience removes the focus from what you want your spouse to do and places the focus squarely where it should be: on what you are doing. Suffering—dying to oneself for the good of someone else—reenacts the gospel. Passionate patience reflects a willingness to suffer for the sake of someone else and trusting God to work in that other person. Show your spouse you are passionate about them and that you will gently and actively wait for as long as it takes to arrive on the same page.

But suffering for the sake of guilting your spouse amounts to nothing more than self-loathing, prideful, moral asceticism. *True sacrifice arises solely from a place of love and enduring commitment.* Passionate patience requires heart-wrenching, soul-searching introspection. Ask yourself difficult questions geared toward a more active waiting.

- How are you changing?
- What financial sacrifices have you made?
- What lines have you drawn in your own life to promote fiscal responsibility and marital fidelity?
- How have you put your spouse's needs above your own in a dramatic, consistent way over a long period of time?
- Have you treated or spoken to your spouse with the tempered steel of virtue when dealing with or talking about finances?

- You are and always have been willing to make sacrifices for your family, but are you really willing to change your relationship with money? Especially if your spouse does not change?

Passionate patience alerts you to the moment when God softens your spouse's heart and prepares the way for a pivotal conversation about money. With passionate patience, you will, through your own small changes and continued movement, arouse your spouse to join you on a journey toward financial health and oneness. With passionate patience, your change in attitude toward money, coupled with your change in attitude toward your spouse over time, moves both of you to the same financial page.

Our friend Joy McClain, author of *Waiting for His Heart: Lessons from a Wife Who Chose to Stay*, knows passionate patience prevails. After decades of struggle, her husband abandoned addiction and chose her, returning to his marital vows. Joy passionately waited. God showed up. More than one reader of *Slaying the Debt Dragon* emailed to share the beginnings of a solo debt-slaying journey. Their once skeptical spouses jumped on board after witnessing the effects of passionate patience. Even in our own story, Cherie and I got on the same page only after I waited patiently while first changing my own spending and money management habits.

Financial Foreplay Tips for Getting on the Same Page

There are some basic steps you can take while actively waiting for your spouse. Your personal changes speak volumes without words about the depth of your love for your spouse, your willingness to sacrifice, and your long-term commitment to financial improvement.

1. **Cut up your credit card.** Studies show you spend up to 50 percent more when you use credit as opposed to cash.[7] Especially if you have been a traditional proponent of plastic, this communicates a change and your commitment to your spouse. Slicing and dicing what's in your wallet eradicates the ability to spend money you don't have.
2. **Stop buying the habitual latte.** If your regular habit costs money, whether coffee, soda, or a favorite magazine subscription, quietly make a change.
3. **Read books about personal finance.** Eliminating extra spending works wonders, but adding positive habits to your life helps just as much. If don't have money to buy a book, check one out from the library. Don't know where to begin? Check out my list of favorite reads in the *Your Money, Your Marriage* Online Guide (found at www.yourmoneyyourmarriage.com/guide).
4. **Invest in your spouse.** Find ways to serve and support the growth of your husband or wife. Investing in their spiritual, physical, and emotional growth leads to positive choices in other areas of life, including finance and romance. Part of my job as a husband allows me the privilege to serve Cherie so that she is the best version of Cherie she can be. Serve your spouse in the same way.
5. **Let every word spoken from your lips be in love.** Before you speak, pause and reflect on how the words you are using about your finances may affect your spouse. Understand that the two of you process information differently.
6. **Accept that you may be the problem.** Getting on the same page with money may require you to move. Do not operate under the assumption that your spouse must move

to your page. Your page is not more important than your marriage or your spouse.

7. **Set the mood.** Create environments, present facts, and communicate in a way that encourages your reluctant spouse to engage in your shared fiscal life.
8. **Do not manipulate.** Manipulation is not the mission. Manipulation never changes the heart and fails to promote real change.
9. **Switch frames.** Financial education does not lead to financial transformation. Instead of educating your spouse, frame your money picture differently. Phrases like, "I need your help" and "Let's do this together" go much further than "Here's what you need to know" or "Here's what you're going to do."

Actions Speak Louder Than Words: Cherie

Andrew Carnegie said, "As I grow older, I pay less attention to what men say. I just watch what they do."[8] Words bounce in and out of our ears all day long. We scroll through our feeds, reading the updates of friends. We flip on Netflix, catching up on the dialogue between our favorite characters. Musical lyrics float through the air and into our brains. We give directives to our kids and speak words of encouragement to a friend. We talk and talk to moms, mentors, or counselors, airing our grievances and attempting to work out our problems. Sometimes no more words remain and at other times no matter what we say or how we say it, our message falls on deaf ears.

Perhaps it's most important in these moments to stop talking for a while, take a deep breath, and then make a move. Talk is essential to a healthy marriage and yet sometimes, talk is cheap. Words spill out of our mouths and, due to their own personal mental blocks or past broken promises, our spouses can't hear or receive them. We need to *do* something.

Brian made plenty of convincing arguments when he began casting the vision of paying off all our debt. I heard very few of them. However, one simple action inched me closer to the idea. One day he told me he had decided to no longer carry our one active credit card in his wallet; he instead placed it in a desk drawer. After all, we *only* had that particular credit card for emergencies. An emergency was unlikely to arise at Home Depot or the drive-through of Taco Bell. So if we really did need to use it, we'd have access to it. However, he placed a deliberate distance between his wallet and the temptation to buy something we could not afford. Brian's fond of the expression, "If you play with snakes, you're bound to get bit," and this simple act of financial subversion effectively removed a rattler from his front right pocket.

Note: Brian did not hold a ceremony where he dramatically snipped our credit cards into a million little pieces. He didn't blow up that Target Visa with firecrackers or place it on a railroad track, allowing a locomotive to roll over it. Brian didn't make a big deal out of it with a speech *nor* did he force me to take the same actions. As a result, his small, quiet gesture spun around in my head for days.

About a month later, during a moment at home alone, I slipped the matching credit card out of my wallet and slid it in the desk drawer alongside his. From there on out, I refused to turn back. I never carried a credit card in my wallet again. We moved from different books to the same page by closing that faux cherry wood drawer with the floppy brass handle. Eventually we canceled the account and cut up those cards without fanfare. But for Brian's first action step, we might have remained enslaved by credit card debt.

While words are essential to financial foreplay, actions lead to true transformation.

I suppose you might think, *That's all well and good for you two. But, we don't even have a credit card to place in a random household drawer.* No worries. Over the years, I compiled a list of actions both husbands and wives could *do* for each other while paying off debt. Honestly though, they're smart measures for any married couple, regardless of their current financial situation, to grow and strengthen a healthy relationship. We'll begin with the fellas. However, ladies don't tune out. Your list of ideas follows.

Action Steps for Husbands to Foster Financial Foreplay

Take Her Out

Spending time together doesn't require spending cash. In fact, some of our most memorable dates cost the least amount of money. Taking a walk, watching a movie we chose together at the library, or going to the grocery store and picking out a half gallon of ice cream are all things we did and are viable options for you too.

Surprise Her

Keeping to a strict budget may seem like you're tossing spontaneity out the window. After all, there are no whirlwind, last-minute romantic getaways when all of your extra dollars are devoted to paying off debt or saving for a specific goal. But you don't have to bring home pricey flowers or some mass-marketed piece of jewelry from the mall. Think simple. Write a note and leave it in the seat of her car. Do a load of laundry. Write words of love with sidewalk chalk in the driveway. Leave a heart with your initials on the steamy bathroom mirror. Don't reserve small messages and tokens of love only for holidays or birthdays. Sprinkle them throughout your everyday lives together.

Turn Off the TV

Six years separate our daughters. Yet at one point during each of their years as a toddler, they did the exact same thing. Both of them hugged the large box in our living room and exclaimed, "I love you, TV," when they were around the age of three. Can we say parenting fail? I know. TV and its little streaming friends provide a release for us all after a long, stressful day. But sometimes, it's good to turn it off. Note: this is best received if you turn off the TV during a show of your own choosing, not of hers. Fix a snack together, play a game, talk about childhood memories. There's plenty to do instead of zoning out. Staring into each other's eyes always leads to deeper intimacy. Staring at the television typically leads to falling asleep on the couch.

Tell Her You Love and Appreciate Her

I know I said this section would focus on actions over words. However, I would be remiss if I didn't tuck away this little piece of wisdom on the list. Weighty money conversations tend to focus on dos and don'ts. Daily conversations are detail-laden by necessity. After all, if we didn't share those important dates and times, our kids would get left behind at school and no one would eat. However, it is important to regularly remind your wife how much you value her.

When we first began paying off debt and getting on the same page with our finances, Brian worked long hours. As a stay-at-home mom, I felt like I added little to the process. It's fairly easy to dismiss your role when all you see are dirty diapers for miles and piles of laundry to the ceiling. When Brian was bold enough to step in and say, "Thank you for stretching the grocery budget to make this meal" or "I love that you've committed to taking care of our kids full-time," my heart sang. Not every woman chooses the same path. She may stay home, work from home, or work outside the home. But all women need to know that what they're doing matters and that their husbands treasure them. Saying "I love you and I appreciate you" once a day is the starting line, not the finish.

Help Her Have Time to Herself

Likely you fell in love with the woman who shares your bed and checking account because of her unique spirit. Married life and motherhood sometimes chip her uniqueness away, as calendars fill with appointments, to-do lists, and obligations. You can actively show love for your wife by encouraging her to do things that feed her soul. For some women this may look like a girls' night; for others it could just be enough time to quietly shower without little fingers poking underneath the bathroom door. A solitary cup of coffee with a good book or a five-mile run have been some of my personal favorites over the last nineteen years of marriage. Help her refresh her soul and watch it renew your marriage.

Every marriage is uniquely different, and each wife has her own needs. But hopefully these generalized ideas provide a launching pad for husbands looking to get creative and step up their "actions speak louder than words" game.

Action Steps for Wives to Foster Financial Foreplay

Show Him Some Love

Your husband craves affection. Consistent physical touch combined with words of affirmation express your true feelings. Steal a kiss when no one is watching. Whisper "I love you" in his ear. Give him a little pinch or a pat as he walks by. Tell him he's doing a great job as a husband, a father, and a friend. Your actions encourage him toward greatness and inspire deeper connection.

Take Interest in His Interests

Thankfully, you and your husband aren't identical twins. Your interests and passions vary. Invest in your guy by studying up on his favorite pastime. Study up on sports, hunting, cars, home repair, or whatever else floats his boat. Impress him with your knowledge or simply spend time together doing what he enjoys. When you take interest in his interests, you show him that what he loves matters to you and that he matters to you too.

Risk Being Risqué

Tap into your adventurous spirit. Spontaneity and initiating romance builds anticipation and enhances intimacy. Send him a saucy text in the middle of the day. Sneak your underthings into his bag. Flash him when he doesn't expect it. Write out your plan for romance and then follow through. Greet him at the door wearing a big smile and little else. Aim to make him blush or surprise him. He'll be excited to see you, and you'll probably both giggle a little, but random acts of flirtation lead to spicy romance.

Affirm His Vocation

Just like you, your husband longs to know that what he does matters. For some men, career choice and life's work hold great weight. It's easy for us all to get caught up in the day-to-day of life without acknowledging the long hours our spouse puts in at work. Show your gratitude for his contribution to your household by writing a note. Recognize the difficulty of his job. Confirm he makes a difference through his actions at work and at home. Boost his spirits and communicate thankfulness. Validate his profession. Your affirmation improves his attitude toward the daily grind and helps him realize he counts.

Tell Him How You Feel

If you are feeling something, you have to tell your husband. Take the time to communicate your emotions, even if you are discouraged or scared or confused or overwhelmed. Look him in the eyes and speak the words you want him to know. Let him know specifically how he can help you. Your husband longs to know what he can do to love you well. Help him understand with your words. Move beyond casual conversation and take action by diving deeper. Begin a path to clear and loving communication with your spouse by being honest and vulnerable.

Again, there are plenty of other ways to relay your love to your guy. His needs are as varied and unique as your own. But move beyond saying something and actually *do* something.

Careful Communication

A few years ago we began the process of running all our communication through a filter. We asked ourselves a simple, clear-cut question.

Is it loving or is it lipping off?

Is what I'm going to say contributing to the wholeness of my spouse? Will my words build them up? Am I valuing God's creation and plan in my treatment of my husband/wife? Or am I merely letting off steam, putting the other person in their place, and satisfying my need to be right. It's not rocket science or a revolutionary thought, but this uncomplicated filter was a game changer for us . . . most days.

We are far from perfect when it comes to communication, and we're sure our children will be able to document this fact for years to come. We still fall short, misunderstand each other, and even mistreat one another with our words. It's easy to make mistakes when you spend so much time together on a regular basis.

Don't deceive yourself into thinking everyone else is nailing this communication (or even this marriage) thing while you and your mate flounder. But knowing you're imperfect (and that your spouse is too) when it comes to communication isn't enough. We all need to move toward changing our patterns and behaviors so we grow closer to each other.

If we want to be on the same financial page, we have to communicate with each other. And the effective communication skills we develop foster financial foreplay. Moving from different books to the same page requires patience and intentionality. Being patient and intentional doesn't just help you balance the books; it brings satisfaction in the bedroom. Knowing each other's needs and telling each other what you want are principles that not only boost your financial outlook but also crank up the heat under the sheets.

Discussion Questions

1. Do you remember waiting for your spouse on your wedding day? Where were you and how did it feel?
2. Have you ever played a game like Win, Lose, or

Draw where you needed to convey a message without speaking? Were you successful? How does our body language, tone, and context make or break financial discussions in marriage?

3. What's the longest you've ever waited in line (think amusement park, concerts, purchasing something, or at a restaurant)?
4. Has exercising patience ever paid off for you in your finances? When has your spouse been patient for you?
5. Which of the action steps to foster financial foreplay have made an impact on your marriage in the past? Which should you be more intentional about on a regular basis?
6. How might the filter of "Is it loving or is it lipping off" rearrange the words you speak to your spouse?

Fostering Financial Foreplay

- Choose one of the action steps to foster financial foreplay and focus on implementing it every day this week.
- Brian and Cherie talked about how big dreams fueled their journey of paying off debt. Brainstorm a list of big financial dreams with your spouse: paying off debt, going on vacation, buying a new house, saving for retirement, paying for your kids' college. Write them down on a large sheet of paper. Stand on that page together and pray over your dreams.

CHAPTER 4

Did You Say Divorce?

From Growing Apart to Being Planted Together

You can't win an argument. You can't because if you lose it, you lose it; and if you win it, you lose it.

DALE CARNEGIE

We sat on the couch watching the national news, barely paying attention. Most of the headlines passed by without us noticing. As the broadcast personality closed the thirty-minute program, he introduced a special-interest story. His droll expression indicated the network's attempt to either restore hope in humanity or at least bring a smile to the viewer's face.

As the news package reeled, the segment about a man and a woman who lived in a rental home in Utah enthralled us. While the husband was away for the evening, a giant boulder rolled down a nearby slope, smashing through the master bedroom wall. The wife, sleeping on her husband's side of the bed, escaped death but still suffered some serious breaks, bumps, and bruises. If she had been on her side of the bed, the result would have been catastrophic. And then the husband spoke. He didn't talk about how glad he was that his wife survived, nor did he discuss the freakish accident. Instead, he spoke words sounding a lot like the silly arguments we've had over the years.

"I kept telling her that boulder was going to roll down the hill."

It was the greatest "I told you so" in history. Laughing, we looked at each other, knowing either one of us might have expressed the same sentiment. None of us marry a carbon copy of ourselves. Husbands and wives collide in opinions when it comes to brand names, toilet paper roll positioning, and television tastes. We repeat our differing viewpoints to each other on loop. Sometimes the result is comical, but most days, whether we realize it or not, we initiate a small fracture in our relationships. We focus in on faults, forgetting the miracle of our marriage. We nitpick and criticize.

We didn't judge boulder guy, because we knew narratives like his go on in the walls of our home too. Besides, for all we know the network could have edited out loving words of concern to get better ratings. But boulder guy exemplifies the ways we can allow our individual viewpoints to separate our hearts. The conflict begins small but widens over time. It's easier than you realize to end up with a boulder suddenly and unexpectedly crashing through the wall of your marriage.

As an attorney, one of the most common phrases Brian hears

in his office is, "We just grew apart." Couples contemplating divorce often feel their relationship is splintered beyond repair and in many cases their finances have spiraled out of control. Neither individual seems to realize that their actions diminished intimacy. But no one really just "grows apart." There's no mysterious force separating hearts and bodies. Years of battling over money often contributed to many of their woes.

Husbands and wives are wired differently. They're also human, which means they will mess up. No matter how hard we try, we will have conflict in our relationships. However, there are things we should and should not say to each other in the midst of arguments. As couples we must take a stand, endeavoring together to nurture our sacred bonds. We need strategies to healthfully move through conflict to strengthen our marriages, leaving the option of divorce and "growing apart" far behind.

Trash Stacking: Brian

Even with a high field-goal percentage, I probably shouldn't be jump-shooting all of my trash into the garbage can. Instead, if I'm throwing something away, I carefully stack the trash as high as possible in a Jenga-style balancing act. Cherie, on the other hand, will smash trash like a human compactor. I will continue with my stacking. She will continue with her smashing. Even though I'm a trash stacker and she's a trash smasher, we have something in common.

Neither one of us likes to take out the trash.

Every day we risk pushing a trash bag to its weight limit and flirt with disaster.

After nineteen years of marriage, our waste management habits haven't caused a blowup (yet). But something as simple as how you handle garbage could be a source of conflict in your marriage. Conflict in marriage is inevitable and isn't necessarily unhealthy. As renowned author Dr. Greg Smalley said, "In marriage conflict is not the problem. Combat is the problem."[1] Conflict brings growth. Combat brings casualties.

Needling each other incessantly over time ends in combat and drives couples apart. Disagreements that seem silly from an outsider's perspective can cause immense conflict in marriage. Couples dispute how toilet paper should hang from the roll (over the top, you monster), what ketchup brand to buy (Heinz for life), and where to squeeze the toothpaste (wherever, just brush 'em). As an aside, the debate is usually whether the toothpaste should be squeezed from the bottom of the tube or if it is all right to squeeze from the middle. Someone in our house is twisting the tube. There's an ongoing investigation.

This may come as a shock to you, but married people fight about money. Just like trash stackers and trash smashers, money personalities take different forms. Perhaps the most common recipe for conflict arises between spenders and savers. How we classify and characterize different approaches to personal finance determines the difference between success and failure. Both the spender and the saver must refrain from categorizing the other. A spender's temptation is to refer to the saver as: a hoarder, a miser, boring, nerdy, no fun, or even controlling. A saver's temptation is to refer to the spender as: irresponsible, flighty, impulsive, out of control, reckless, or even dangerous. When tempted, both view the other as an enemy.

Your different approaches to money can allow your marriage to thrive; they do not have to be a hindrance. Avoid characterizing your spouse's money tendencies in a way that devalues them. *Dropping labels raises intimacy in your marriage.* You can't initiate financial foreplay by name-calling, which is what labeling your spouse a shopaholic or a tightwad really is. Accurate or not, nobody likes to be called names. Approach your shared financial lives in a way that exemplifies your joint efforts, not your differences. Move from "he's the spender and I'm the saver" to "we're a couple that works together."

Beyond name-calling, labeling the other spouse serves as an excuse for financial failure. Ultimately, you're blaming your spouse for all your money problems and shirking your own responsibility. Marriages where couples blame each other are marriages that end in shambles. Departing from blame and name-calling eliminates conflicts and focuses couples on the actual issue, which has nothing to do with who's the spender and who's the saver.

The real issue is: somebody's gotta take out the trash.

With finances, taking out the trash means husbands and wives remove unwarranted expectations of each other. Each of us needs to stop stacking on problems and stop smashing problems out of sight.

How to Stop Stacking and Smashing

"Stop, collaborate, and listen." Vanilla Ice. Spotting the real issue requires stepping away from the conflict altogether and looking at it through an objective lens. Work with your spouse; ask lots of why questions. Be willing to answer the same questions. Listen patiently to one another with a spirit of resolution, not argument. Perhaps your spouse longs to move to a new house. Rather than immediately shutting them down, ask why in order to see things from their point of view. Really listen. Keep asking clarifying questions until you understand.

Change your language. "Your debt," "my money," "my retirement account," and "your overdraft fees" are all divisive phrases. They are also incorrect. On a car ride to buy a Mother's Day gift for Cherie, my daughter summed this concept up well. "Dad, if a boy wants to marry me and he has student loans, he's going to need to pay those off before we get married."

"Why's that?" I inquired.

"Because before we get married, those are his loans. After we get married, they are ours." She was eight years old and wise beyond her years. When you're married, it's all "ours."

Enlist a third party. Once we identified that the real trash-stacking/trash-smashing issue was taking out the garbage, the solution was clear. We didn't reach a compromise or negotiate a fair arrangement; we instructed our teenage daughter, Anna, to start taking out the trash. This was a good solution for us. But for you, Anna would charge her hourly rate plus mileage, so it is an impractical choice to resolve conflict in your home; another third party might help. Warning: a third party does not determine who is right or who is wrong. A third party does not mean an unscientific Facebook or Twitter poll. A helpful third party possesses the experience and wisdom necessary to sift through the argument and diagnose the source of controversy. Your momma, your golf buddy, and your BFF are terrible third parties. Neutrality, distance, and expertise mark quality choices. Pastors, counselors, or maybe your money mentors (more on that later) make better third-party help.

Remember what's important. Over the course of our marriage, I've relied on these five critical conflict resolution maxims. These tenets helped me put life in perspective and moved us closer together in situations that could have torn us apart.

- Your spouse comes before everything else.
- Your marriage is more important than your money.
- Love trumps winning an argument every time.
- Moving toward your spouse in your finances moves you closer to your spouse.
- Your example speaks louder than harsh words.

What to Do When You've Stepped in It: Cherie

Our premarital counseling experience was less than ideal, despite having no fewer than three pastors involved with our wedding (hey—go big or go home). Each of the ministers had flourishing congregations, one had a second job, and none of them really had time to meet with us on a regular basis.

So we settled for reading a couple of books together on our own and a sit-down session with one of the pastors and his wife. A little too bright-eyed and green around the gills, we nestled together on the couch as they peppered us with trick questions about each other, our relationship, and our envisioned future.

The entire time, we kept glancing nervously at each other. It wasn't because we were uncertain about our decision to marry. Honestly, it didn't have anything to do with the odd counseling session, its slightly uncomfortable questions, and even less comfortable lumpy couch.

No, we were giving each other the stink eye, because something. smelled. *awful.*

Naturally, each of us assumed it was the other. What *did* we eat for dinner before we came? Brian stared me down with an expression that conveyed "Cherie, for real?!" I glared back "Seriously, Brian?"

Then together our suspicions shifted to the pastor and his

wife. They were kind, but maybe the pastor had worn his boots for ten years too long? Or perhaps a horse was living in the spare bedroom? Regardless of the source, we were ready to escape Smellville Penitentiary as quickly as we could. As soon as we sensed a lull in the conversation, we capitalized on the opportunity to excuse ourselves and sprinted toward fresh air and freedom.

The open air brought relief but was frigid. We hopped in the car, slammed on the gas, and cranked up the heat. Then there it was again. The same horrid stench filled the space around us. The car's heater provided no respite as it merely circulated and intensified the unrelenting odor we were attempting to flee. We both gagged and looked around: at each other, at the cabin of the vehicle, out the windows. It was a pitch-black night. Where was the unforgiving stank coming from?

After what felt like an eternity (in reality less than two minutes), Brian muttered: "I think it must be me."

Dry heaving, I exclaimed, "Roll down the windows! Turn the heater off!"

Less than a mile down the country road, we pulled over. Brian determined he had really stepped in it at our counseling session. There was dog poop all over one of his dress shoes. From inside the car, I watched as he scraped his shoe (still on his foot) on the post of a stop sign—the very same stop sign at the T in the road where he began counting for the fifth house on the right.

When he returned to the car, the stink was a little better, but still not great. We decided his footwear needed more focused attention. By this time we were close to my grandmother's house. We stopped in for a quick visit with the hopes of scoring some bleach wipes. My grandma Beulah came to the door in her housecoat, welcoming us in, and of course offering a snack because that's what grandmas do.

"Um, Grandma? We think Brian may have stepped in some dog poop and needs to clean off his shoe."

Grandma Beulah, a girl raised in the backwoods of Kentucky, wasn't exactly prim and proper. I'm still not sure how she managed to snatch Brian's shoe off his foot, pull it to her nose to sniff, and no-nonsensically proclaim, "Yep, that's just a little bit of dog poo" in one swift motion. And that's how my elderly grandmother ended up cleaning poop off my fiancé's shoe in the middle of a cold January night.

From time to time, each of us steps in it. We make mistakes. We say words we shouldn't have. We cross a line. We snap back. What can we do, though, when things have gone too far and we realize we have metaphorical poop on our shoes?

While you may not have a down-home grandma ready to take the mess off your hands, you can begin the cleanup. Probably the most challenging part of marriage is owning our stuff—the errors and blunders, the harsh words, and sometimes downright stupidity. But we can't be cowards when it comes to admitting when we've blown it and subsequently asking for forgiveness.

The two words I need to say more often in my marriage and actually mean them?

I'm sorry.

I'm not sure what it is about these two small words that cause me to cower with fear and bristle with pride at the same time. I'm excellent at complaining, blaming, and comparing. But owning my mistakes? Apparently, I didn't inherit Grandma Beulah's poop-cleaning gene.

Apologizing and then cleaning up any chaos we've created in our relationships requires courage. Making things right necessitates humility. If you're never willing to be honest about your own faults and/or mistakes, you'll never experience the intimacy that comes as a result. Grinding our teeth and dragging our feet leave us on separate sides of the bed, both cold and isolated. Admitting our own faults grows roots in our marriage.

I suppose it would be easy to see apologizing as a sign of weakness. And I realize no argument or marital conflict is completely one-sided. It takes two to tango (and tangle, for that matter). But being brave by surrendering our need to win an argument typically softens the other person and beckons them to a similar positioning of the heart.

Saying "I'm sorry" comes with great risk. You're not guaranteed a reciprocal response. We place ourselves in a vulnerable position. But should that matter? We shouldn't ask for forgiveness or apologize only to hear the same words in reply. With courage, we should acknowledge our shortcomings because we long for the transformation of our souls and our marriages.

The best piece of advice I took from our smelly premarital counseling was a simple prayer I've prayed throughout the years over our marriage. The pastor's wife said in passing that for decades she had prayed the same words herself in times of conflict and stress.

"God, change my husband's heart or change mine."

The quick sentence isn't a magical incantation or miracle spell. Uttering it doesn't yield instantaneous change either. However, this straightforward invocation ushers God into our conflicts. Our arguments and disagreements shrink as we long for divine intervention to reshape our marriage. *Invite God into the middle of your mess.* Over the years, when I would inhale a large breath to unleash a vicious utterance on Brian during a fight, these words began to weave their way through my soul. They knock through my heart and rattle through my brain.

Change our hearts, God. Not just his, not just mine, but our hearts together. Bring us closer—to You, to each other. In our humanity, do something supernatural. Show up in a way that only You could. Take two shattered and confused hearts and meld them into one. Embolden me with the words of truth to own my sin. Strengthen me to say "I'm sorry" when I need to, regardless of Brian's response. Help me to go first, not because it's what's best for my husband or my marriage, but because it's what You call me to do—to lay down my own selfish desires and put You and others first.

We all step in it. We all miss the mark and blow it. We all cause a stink. In the context of marriage, may you be brave enough, strong enough, and beautiful enough to go first when it comes to saying you're sorry and righting your wrongs.

Tending: Brian

A handful of years ago, I discovered Mel Bartholomew's square foot gardening, an organic raised-bed method to grow your own produce. My grandfathers both harvested bountiful crops from their massive vegetable gardens, and I resolved to take advantage of my predisposed genetic agricultural giftedness. So I ordered and devoured Mel's book on square foot gardening. It turns out, my grandpas' green thumbs developed from arduous farm labor with archaic tools in the early 1900s and not from ordering a glossy how-to book on Amazon from the comfort of a recliner.

Using clearance wood from the local big-box hardware store, I fashioned 2" x 6" boards into a four-foot square. Underneath the open area of the square, I laid dense weed cloth and, for good measure, covered the area with several layers of newspaper and cardboard. My favorite premise of square foot gardening is that it requires minimal weed removal. The backbreaking effort of pulling weeds previously discouraged me from ever planting anything. This extreme weed aversion culminated in the making of my own soil. Yes, dirt is plentiful where I live, but by controlling the ingredients of the ground, I reckoned weeds didn't stand a chance. Using a hand rake to thoroughly mix the amount of soil required to fill a 4' x 4' garden bed proved exhausting and filthy but strangely satisfying.

Not long after carefully planting my seeds, I reveled in victory as basil, cilantro, and tomatoes thrived in my homemade veggie plot. In the beginning, an occasional weed appeared, but the shallow soil allowed me to quickly remove it. But then, as the weather seems to do in the Midwestern summer, it became unbearably hot. When I constructed the beds in early spring, I failed to contemplate how much I despise being outside in the summer heat. Daily tending turned into casually watching from the window and waving hello. I wished my plant friends good luck without me, still hoping for a great harvest.

The cardboard and newspaper decomposed. Weed cloth, no matter the density, withered in fright at the unspeakable evil perpetrated by my yard's despicable and unyielding weeds lurking just below the ground's surface. By the end of summer, a supposed impenetrable fortress fell to the enemy it was designed to prevent. Dreams of fresh veggies died, and our yard forever bears remnants of crushed hope in the shape of a square outline where now no grass will grow.

Growing a garden is a lot like growing a marriage. If you don't tend your garden, it will die. If you don't tend your marriage, it will die. When struggling married couples say they just grew apart, I think of my garden and the harvest that could have been. Saying that I never intended for my garden to be overgrown is a lie. Every day, I elected to ignore my garden's progress due to the heat or some other lame excuse. I made several conscious decisions. Couples don't accidentally grow apart; couples intentionally choose different directions.

It begins simply enough. Couples don't listen to each other, distracted by technology or media. They fail to schedule time together because they're overworked and overcommitted. Askew priorities cause one or both individuals to place other things—hobbies, friends, work, and even their children—above their spouse. Their deepest level of intimacy devolves into a casual wave hello in the morning.

Being planted together takes more than one day of colossal effort. Everything is more exciting and motivating in the beginning. When the heat turns up and circumstances become difficult, we must continue nurturing each other as we did in the beginning. We also need to give due regard to a proper foundation. When I read the book about square foot gardening, I skipped over the parts about the painstaking steps to prep the ground below. The instructions advised me to eliminate all vegetation before laying down the newspaper, weed cloth, and soil. Always build your garden, and your marriage, on a pure foundation. Instead of clearing the ground, I spent the majority of my time making the soil because that was active and it resembled work. But activity does not equal productivity. Had I just taken time before mixing the soil to observe and remove all threats to my garden, I'd be making you salsa right now.

Weeds didn't just come up from the bottom of the garden bed. In the spring, I deliberately mowed my lawn in a particular direction, with deference to wind conditions as to avoid any cross contamination. But because of my disdain for hot summer days and working in the open sun, once the temperature rose, I mowed like a madman and littered my precious beds with weed and grass debris. In the beginning, I watered my veggies at designated hours. But once the heat became unbearable, I let the plants shrivel and crossed my fingers for rain.

We often operate the same way in our marriages. As newlyweds, we are gentle, tender, and considerate. As the years pass, we take our spouses for granted and lose the delicate balance required for growing together. Whether it be the hurry of life or general inattentiveness, we cause our spouses to wither with our harsh words or unrealistic demands—usually when combustible circumstances like money or sex ignite in our lives. Underestimating the forces working against your marriage results in a relationship overrun with complications like a garden overrun with weeds. Tend to your spouse no matter your present external circumstances. Sacrifice your time and effort for one another, even if the situation seems unbearable. Choose to grow together. Water your souls by drinking from the same well through reading God's Word together and praying for one another. Pay attention to each other's needs and commit to meeting those needs. Have fun together. Go dancing. Hold hands. Make out. Do considerate acts for each other like you did when your love was new. By so doing, you will reap a bountiful and satisfying harvest now and for years to come.

Safe Words: Cherie

We were in the pharmacy, waiting to pick up a prescription. To put it mildly, it had been a rough week. Brian's job (like most jobs) demands a high level of excellence, bringing with it a high level of stress. Worn out and tired, he wondered out loud if his blood pressure would reflect his stress level. He wandered over to the standard automated blood pressure cuff in the waiting area and plopped down to take a measurement. Surprisingly, it wasn't too high, but it was borderline.

"Are those things even accurate?" I scoffed as I scooted him out of the way and took his spot. I placed my arm in the cuff and waited patiently for my own result. A low resting pulse and low blood pressure are badges of honor for me. I must be medically narcissistic, but I take delight in medical professionals gushing over my healthy vitals. As my stats rolled in, I anticipated landing in the lower portion of green, signaling my excellent health.

Except that's not what happened. I gazed in shock as my measurements registered through the roof, far outpacing Brian's borderline blood pressure. Bright red blazed back as my blood pressure landed in the danger zone. I still doubted the results, but a call to a nurse friend and a doctor's appointment revealed the truth. My physician-pleasing days were over. My blood pressure required medicine to keep me from becoming the mom in the American Heart Association commercials who chirps, "I'm fine," and then keels over with a cardiac episode.

Prevention in any area of our lives keeps a minor situation from morphing into a major one. Whether through lifestyle changes or other interventions, changes in our routine keep our hearts from failing and our feet from stumbling. This certainly rings true in marriage. Harmoniously solving a conflict in the middle of the conflict just doesn't happen. But we can place safeguards on our relationships or preventive practices that minimize fighting, especially when it comes to money.

Every married couple needs "safe words" that promote smart finance and spicy romance. I'm not going where you think I'm going with this one, by the way. We all need code words or phrases that keep arguments from escalating. When I was a kid, my mom employed this practice when my brother and I began to bicker in public. She'd whisper *finito* (Italian for "it's all done") in our ears and we knew we'd better knock it off quickly or there would be a price to pay.

The words you choose are up to you. A married couple on a sitcom we watched employed the word *pause* to keep a fight from going too far. We've often used the twenty-second time-out basketball gesture—double tapping both shoulders lightly—to keep us from saying something we shouldn't say. Your safe words keep disagreements from turning into an irreparable rift caused by spur-of-the-moment anger. Think of your words as preventative medicine.

Actions can serve as safe words too, ensuring you won't stumble into dangerous territory. My friend Tricia knows her husband's blood sugar dives when he hasn't had enough to eat. After years of experience, and a few conflicts that could have been avoided, she began to make sure he had plenty to eat before she brought up topics of conversation that could lead to a disagreement. Hunger was a trigger for him. It might be for you too. Or you may struggle with other outside factors that cause a small disagreement to progress into an otherwise avoidable fight or worse.

It's wise for couples to employ the HALT acronym to avoid damaging arguments. Don't begin a money discussion if either of you is Hungry, Angry, Lonely, or Tired. Make it your practice to take a deep breath and evaluate both your current state of mind and that of your spouse. It's okay to disagree about how you handle money, but it's not okay to pile hateful words on each other in the middle of your debate. A quick HALT prevents venomous words from tripping off the tongue. A calm demeanor also neutralizes potentially delicate situations.

As Lieutenant Commander Rorke Denver says, "Calm is contagious."[2] Safe words usher calm into conflict. When one party de-escalates, the other tends to do the same. Combative words cause more friction, and name-calling of any variety rankles with dissension. Thinking about how you will fight before you fight protects the heart of your marriage. Long before an argument ensues, it's smart to define parameters to guard your relationship from potential damage. Safe words and actions aren't guaranteed to stop a fight from occurring but could keep one from spiraling out of control.

Even though it took great humility for me to admit the days of bragging about my superior vitals were over, I'm glad I sat down to check my blood pressure in the pharmacy. I didn't have any other symptoms often connected with elevated blood pressure levels. But within my body was a quiet, ticking time bomb. Left unchecked, I could have landed in the hospital or worse. In each of our marriages, the silent potential for damaging conflict exists. Using safe words works like preventive medicine, protecting our relationships from harm and even death.

Fight Fair

A room filled with married couples in their finest attire laughed as we played goofy icebreakers together. Hundreds of men and women turned out for a local church's prom night for married people. With awesome door prizes on the line, husbands and wives did their best to win each game before the dancing began. The final activity involved a reboot of the old youth group classic "Never Have I Ever."

The evening's emcee asked probing questions of couples, and if either admitted participating in whatever activity he described, those individuals had to sit down. We can't remember any of the questions that cleared the room, narrowing the field to the one remaining woman. However, we do remember the final scenario. It was a silly, throwaway inquiry designed to get the very last person to sit down.

"Never have I ever fought unfair with my spouse."

The entire room giggled at such an outlandish thought. Each person in attendance recognized their tendency toward manipulation and delivering low blows.

However, the woman remained standing. Dumbfounded, the emcee struggled for words and scratched his head. She had already won the game, but perhaps she thought there was a bonus round? She towered over her already seated husband and exclaimed, "I don't fight unfair, do I?" He silently stared back and the crowd awkwardly groaned as she had just indeed fought unfair. The emcee awarded her the grand prize and attempted to restore life to the party.

Because we are all human, we will fall short. You will fight about money with your spouse. That makes you normal. But fighting about money doesn't have to mean growing apart. You can work through the disagreements and differing opinions to find a place of being planted together, rooted in God's plan and purpose for your money and your marriage.

Individuals are unique. We each approach life differently. But those differences don't have to be a curse; they can be a blessing. In fact, our differences are assets, not liabilities. Asking forgiveness and placing your spouse's needs first reboots your efforts and provides another opportunity for success. Tending our marriages allows us to grow together. Instituting safe words weeds out potential problems before they happen.

Employing preventive and strengthening practices saves your money and deepens your intimacy. Once you become intentional about conflict—instead of just letting it happen to you—affection and connection replace confusion and anger.

Discussion Questions

1. Are you a trash stacker or a trash smasher? What's your stance on toilet paper positioning, ketchup brand, and toothpaste squeezing?
2. How have small, and somewhat silly, disagreements taken a toll on your relationship?
3. Remember Brian's unfortunate dog excrement story? What's the grossest thing you've ever stepped in?
4. Why is it so difficult to admit we've made mistakes and to ask for forgiveness?
5. How does inviting God into the mess—the conflict in our marriages—reshape our perspective?

Fostering Financial Foreplay

- Choose an activity to do together—fixing a meal together, going on a walk, making out, holding hands, reading Scripture—that will help you tend to your marriage this week.
- Define safe words for your marriage. What will you say to pause a fight before it goes too far? What actions will you take to make sure that minor conflict doesn't develop into a major argument? What words will you choose not to speak?

CHAPTER 5

Who Leads Your Life?

From Busy to Prioritized

Life is what happens to you while you're busy making other plans.

JOHN LENNON

"We're just so busy!" The American family blurts this constant refrain everywhere from social gatherings to work to church to the awkward moment when you run into someone at the grocery store and don't want to talk. Then comes the inevitable reply: "We are too! You wouldn't even believe it."

It's almost like a continual family comparison game. "Oh yeah? You've got a baseball tournament, soccer practice, and overtime hours? We have a band concert, my mother-in-law's birthday, and a kindergarten graduation."

Sometimes we wear our busyness as a badge of honor. If you're not as busy as we are, we wonder what's wrong with you. Maybe you're not as important as we are. Maybe your kids aren't as gifted. Maybe you're just lazy.

The frenetic pace at which we live leaves us out of breath. We wonder if this "pick up/drop off/post all the fun things we're doing online so everyone can see" existence really is all there is for our families, our marriages, our lives, our souls. Is this as good as it gets?

There will always be demands on your time. You have to work so your family can eat. You must do laundry and clean the house so you don't end up on the next episode of *Hoarders*. Your children need to be educated so they're not living in your basement for the next fifty-five years. It's not even a bad thing for your children to have extracurriculars. It's not a dreadful prospect for you to have life passions either. But let's not kid ourselves. Who did this to you? *Busyness is not something thrust upon us or a circumstance outside of our control. Busyness is a choice.* We choose our activities, and, as a result, we choose the schedule accompanying them. We choose the "just so busy" mantra and then also choose to complain about it like someone else manages our calendars.

Time for a reality check. Busyness kills intimacy in your marriage. When we run at breakneck speed, we barely see one another. Married couples become roommates instead of lovers. And when we actually find a few spare moments to spend together, we fall asleep on the couch before the first episode of that newly released show on Netflix runs its opening credits. Who wants to have a hot night of sex when you can barely keep your eyes open?

I know what you're thinking: *Hang on a minute. I thought this book was supposed to tell me how to manage my money and have a better marriage? I didn't sign up for a lecture on how to spend my time.*

Financial foreplay encompasses more than simply balancing your checkbook so you can get down to business with your spouse. The choices we make for our schedules determine how much money we spend. Those choices in turn may determine how many hours or years we work, what kind of house we live in, and how much we can save for retirement. Choices about our calendars either deplete or increase our finances. Those same choices also deplete or increase our energy levels. The schedules we keep determine whether we share family meals at home or constantly eat in the car. And they indicate how much we value romance and intentional time spent together.

Choices lead your family. The choices you make either lead you down a harried, exhausted road or into a wide-open space where your marriage and family can thrive. Moving your relationship from being busy to being prioritized redirects both your finances and your romance toward flourishing freedom.

Why Putting Together a Grill Doesn't Lead to "Grilling": Brian

I'm not sure why gas grills don't come preassembled or even partly assembled. What I am sure of is that you should never put one together outside, on a humid Midwestern night, in a suit, with your agitated wife, swarmed by bloodthirsty mosquitoes.

We were unusually swamped that summer. Overtime, extra jobs, dishes, laundry, mowing the back forty, swim lessons, other summer kid activities, family obligations, and distractions of all kinds hampered our regular couple time. And then our grill bit the dust. Lest we go without the flamey smoked goodness that highlights our mealtimes, we decided to replace it.

One Friday, I came home later than normal and Cherie again

mentioned the need to go grill shopping. Is that a thing—grill shopping? "Let's go," I said. Somehow I thought we could pick up a grill and put it together all in time for me to have shish kebabs at a decent hour. In record time, we bought this hunk of metal with infrared heat, four burners, and a hot plate. Ignoring the two-person lift warning, I shoved the gargantuan box into our modest-size trunk and scurried home.

Twilight loomed, so I had to hurry. Gravity benefits you when dropping a two-hundred-pound box into a sensible midsize sedan, but it mocks you as you try to reverse this feat. After tearing the rubber seal on our trunk and using a system of leverage that would make Archimedes proud, I delivered the purchase from my car's abyss. Dusk squelched the remaining daylight. I was sweaty. It was, as we call it in Indiana, getting buggy. My face became sullen after I sliced open the box.

It took fewer parts and pieces to put a man on the moon than it would to build this grill. Bags of tiny screws, washers, nuts, knobs, hoses, and bolts, all supposedly different sizes, looked exactly the same—especially in the dark. When you're famished, hurried, sweat-laden, short-sighted, exhausted, irritated, and being attacked by vampire mosquitoes on steroids, asking your wife to let the toddler put herself to bed so she can hold the flashlight is not wise. And demanding the Herculean task of perfectly aiming the light while balancing the massive steel lid hovering over your head as you fiddle around looking for the right screws to use could prove fatal.

At a minimum, I am sure Cherie considered several alibis:

"The lid was just so heavy, officer. Would you like a shish kebab?"

"Yes, those are my fingerprints, but I was inside when I heard the crash. Filet?"

"Are you sure it dropped on him twice? Who wants s'mores?!"

Awesome life tips every couple needs:

1. Putting a grill together at night will test your marriage.
2. Don't test your marriage on purpose.
3. It is my solemn advice to always buy a preassembled grill.

We let the sun set on our anger as our bellies and hearts growled in unison. Let's just say no financial foreplay occurred.

The lesson we learned is when we don't have enough margin in our lives, we end up doing something ridiculous. *Decreased margin in our lives equals increased strain in our marriages.*

In the great grill debacle, we didn't have enough margin and ignored our values, needs, and dreams. Our core values as a couple do not involve bickering or premeditation of various crimes. We need food, but a grill isn't the only way to prepare food. I've dreamed of being in a suit drenched in perspiration, outside with Cherie at midnight; but that dream involved tango lessons and Argentina. That dream ended quite differently than the char-burned verbal blowup in the driveway.

In order to make wise decisions regarding our schedules, we need to first define our values, needs, and dreams. Each aspect connects with and impacts the others. Agreeing on well-defined, immovable, rock-solid principles simplifies decision-making for couples.

Decision-Making Action Steps That Lead to Financial Foreplay

1. Pop popcorn. Or make some type of snack to share.
2. Clear the area. The kids are either in bed or not home at all. The TV is off. Phones are put away.
3. Write down immovable priorities. Exchange, review, and

discuss the lists with your spouse. Listen to one another. While these vary from couple to couple, some of our immovable money and marriage priorities include: growing in our faith together, remaining physically and financially faithful in our marriage, intentionally parenting our kids, paying our taxes, living debt-free, and saving for retirement.

4. Agree on intrinsic needs. Cable television is a want. Running water and hugs are needs. Have an open and honest discussion distinguishing wants and needs. Some of our money and marriage needs include: love, shelter, electricity, affordable transportation, food, clothing, and sex.
5. Imagine a future together. Ask each other what the ideal looks like in the next five, ten, and twenty years.

In this exercise, you are not seeking middle ground. You are hoping for common ground. A shared foundation supports a deeper connection.

Once our values, needs, and dreams are defined, they point us in the right direction and help us make wise choices regarding our scheduled activities.

The Calendar Challenge

Let's take the philosophical principles we established with our values, needs, and dreams and apply them to our actual lives. Take out your monthly calendars. Look through the dates and appointments. You can use the following three questions to help determine if an activity aligns with your priorities.

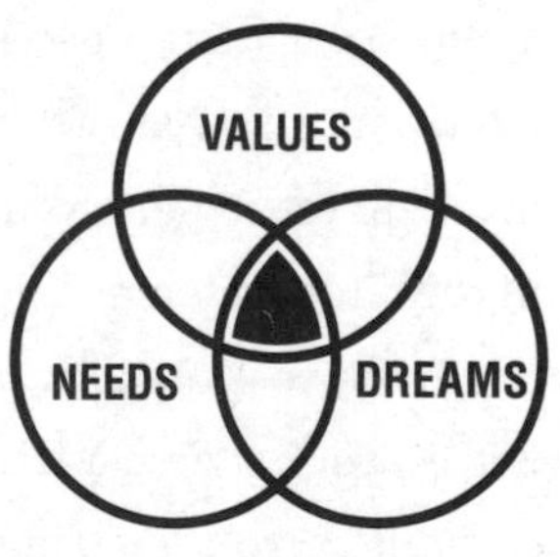

1. Does this option align with our shared values?
2. Does this alternative meet a shared need?
3. Does this course of action progress us toward our shared dreams?

When you both have similar answers to these three questions, your marriage launches toward your dreams. Everyday distractions or detours delay or even derail your dreams. Chip and Dan Heath, authors of the bestselling book *Switch: How to Change Things When Change Is Hard,* offer a poignant suggestion to achieve your desired outcome: "Marry your long-term goal with short-term critical moves."[1] That sounds fine in the abstract, but here's how to wed your everyday routine with your lifelong dreams.

Mark each and every activity with a small V, N, or D to clarify if what you're doing actually fits with your money and your marriage goals. Talk with your spouse about how to remove items from your schedule that don't mesh with your shared vision.

Let's consider a family vacation through this filter. Does going on a vacation align with your shared values? If you both value time together and fun experiences for your kids, it probably does. Does a family vacation meet a shared need? If you need rest and an opportunity to create memories with your children, then it could. Does a family vacation progress us toward our shared dreams? Perhaps. However, if you are trying to get out of debt, save for college, or invest in retirement, you may be compromising long-term dreams in the name of temporary fun.

If you're struggling to decide whether a regular obligation fits within your shared VND, put that activity on pause. Let's say you committed to a knitting class that meets once a week for twelve months or your six-year-old spars twice a week at her Kung Fu dojo. Take a break. After a one-month window, discuss whether you should reinstate the activity on your calendar. If after reevaluation, the interest in Kung Fu, knitting, or (if you're really talented) Kung Fu knitting remains true to your shared VND, put it back on the planner.

Consider adding prioritized appointments to your schedule. Weekly budget meetings, joining a small group, going to marital counseling, intentional couple time, and planned family nights reinforce shared values, needs, and dreams. Place a premium on engagements that align with your long-term goals through purposeful scheduling.

Everybody is busy. Pastor and author John Ortberg described the condition this way: "Being busy is an outer condition; being hurried is a sickness of the soul."[2] Let me be straight with you: *hurried people have hurried sex*. Or they have no sex at all because they're bone-tired. That's no way to live. Margin in our lives safeguards sanctity in the sheets.

The Leader Is Okay: Cherie

When our daughter Anna was three years old, we spent many hours entertained by her antics. Who needs cable TV when you have an unpredictable and creative preschooler? She hosted an impromptu talk show aptly named *The Anna Show* where, if lucky, we were invited to be her special guest stars. This faux television extravaganza featured comedic genius, interviews with stuffed animals, and a recurring bit called "Let's drink!," where guests were expected to hammer down a bottle of water while she chugged her sippy filled with milk. Yes, I am a little terrified of what her college experience might look like. Thank you for reminding me.

We also played countless games of follow-the-leader through our house. We adored her free-spirited shenanigans and often found ourselves following her around our small home, imitating each skip, hop, or tiptoe over and under obstacles she carefully arranged. One Saturday afternoon, as we made our way in a three-person train across the living room toward the kitchen, tutu-clad Anna stepped out onto the slate entryway, and, before we could catch her or even exhale, she brutally face-planted on the floor. Every parent knows that moment of panic when a toddler or small child wipes out or bumps their head or collides with a static object. You stand motionless, holding your breath. You think, *Man, that must have hurt.* And then, if you give in to emotion, you ask three words certain to cause a complete and utter meltdown with flowing tears. "Are you okay?" But sometimes you can catch yourself in the split second before asking that question and instead let the silence take over. By a great miracle of grace, we managed not to say a single word in this one rare instance of parenting.

Breathless, we stood anxiously waiting. Anna's small body prostrate on the ground was motionless. Then in a moment of defiance, her right arm raised up in the air, and a teeny preschool finger pointed to the sky, just like a miniature professional wrestler might do for dramatic effect. With her face still buried in tile, she made the proud, albeit a bit garbled, proclamation, "The leader is okay!" We shared a glance and then giggled, both relieved she was not injured.

It's a message we need to hear from time to time as a married couple. *The leader is okay.* We will be okay. Even when we fall flat on the floor and the hurt and the disappointment sting, life is okay. Forget a perfect marriage; I just want an okay one. I want a marriage where true needs are met and where, even in the midst of the challenges of life, I find a soft place to land and a solid rock on which I can stand. Oh, the leadership lessons you can learn from a pigtailed little girl.

Fast-forward nine years into our story and we're still gaining wisdom from our daughter's experience. Anna the middle schooler chose to play the clarinet in band. Our school doesn't just have a run-of-the-mill band program. Our band is a machine, a championship legacy, and a source of pride for our community. Each year I sat amazed by the level of musicality the students produced in such a short period of time. That excellence didn't just appear from thin air; the conductors cultivated it over time and required their young musicians to commit to practicing regularly. Before one of Anna's very last band concerts, the director, Mr. Kalugyer, beamed with pride when introducing her group, sharing the delight of just how difficult their featured musical selections were to play.

He continued, praising the students for their hard work and their natural talent. But he concluded with a leadership truism that still rings in my ears: "I don't care how good you are. You have to take direction from someone."

It's true for a middle school band, but it's true for your marriage too. No matter how awesome you are—at your job, at life, at being parents, at managing money, even at being married—you still need to take direction from someone. You need a guide to both model for you and counsel you on what it looks like to manage money well and remain married. And if you want to learn how to move from busy to prioritized values, indispensable needs, and shared dreams in your marriage, you need someone who doesn't just talk about living a balanced life, but someone who lives without a harried state of existence.

But how do we know who to turn to for that sort of advice? Who can model what it looks like to balance your money and your marriage? The obvious Sunday school answer is that God speaks to you through the Bible to show you how to live, how to cultivate a healthy marriage, and how to manage money. But I'd argue you need more. You need community.

Specifically, you need money mentors—people who have been where you are and landed where you want to be. While their path might seem mysterious and magical, I can assure you it is not. They understand and can explain how the link between time management and money management leads to financial foreplay. Look for those people who make choices to quell the busyness. They structure their lives in ways that combat the cultural pull for more and more activity and stuff, choosing the exact opposite. Seek out men and women who share an intimate bond with each other. Search for couples who may not have what the world classifies as the dream home or fanciest car or elaborate vacations but remain content nonetheless. These are the voices you need. They have the advice you require. These are the marriage Dan Henrys you need to follow.

I don't care how good you are. You have to take direction from someone.

I can hear you already. "Sure, Cherie, this sounds peachy keen. We'd love to have a couple like this in our lives. But (A) where the heck are we supposed to find them? And (B) you're telling us to quit doing so much. How are we supposed to find time to meet with these imaginary, yet awesome people?"

You're right. Finding someone to mentor you is no easy feat. And finding the time to actually meet with them becomes less easy when you're battling the busy monster. But time spent with money mentors is an investment in your future. Have a sense of urgency about finding someone to coach you. Once you find someone who agrees to help, be intentional about scheduling time with them on a regular basis. It doesn't have to be daily. It doesn't even have to be weekly or monthly. Meet together once every quarter or even twice a year. It's important, probably more important than dozens of other dates on your calendar.

But back to the momentous task of how to find this sagacious and inspiring couple to breathe new life into your marriage. I could be wrong, but I'd hazard a guess you already have someone in mind. They're that couple who isn't fake or perfect. They don't always get along but they do treat one another with respect. They may not be the prettiest and they're definitely not the most extravagant when it comes to the material possessions of their lives. They're less likely to constantly remind you of their undying love for one another on Facebook and more likely to be seen walking hand-in-hand somewhere. They are kind and generous but not showy. You might be related to them, or you might not. You may have known them for years, or perhaps you have just met. Think through the couples in your life whom you admire. Consider the people you know whose lives seem to sing even in the direst circumstances. They're level-headed, even-keeled, steady, and unrocked by drama.

Again, I can hear you. "I've got nothing, Cherie. I know no people like those you have described or at least none I'm comfortable opening up my messy marriage and messy management of time and money with and saying, 'What should I do with all my crazy?'" If you truly don't know anyone who meets this description, I'd recommend asking someone you know and trust to make a suggestion. Turn to your pastor, a counselor, or trusted friends.

As far as feeling uncomfortable about opening up and sharing the state of your marriage, money, time, and souls, you may have the wrong idea about what a money mentor is all about. Instead of seeing a meeting with a money mentor as an opportunity to bare your soul and talk about all of your shortcomings, see it as fulfilling a childhood dream. You see, you get to become a detective. Yes, you may be struggling in your own marriage, and yes, more than likely a money mentor will be able to speak into that struggle, providing both hope and practical solutions. But if you're too nervous to begin with your specific challenges, start by asking questions.

Asking questions diffuses what could be an awkward situation, providing wisdom and counsel along the way. If you really want to know how this couple has managed to remain married for decades, pay off debt, raise awesome children, or, if you're lucky, all of the above, you need to ask them. Don't know where to begin? I've got a few sample questions for you to try on for size.

Questions to Ask Money Mentors:

- What do you do when you fight about money?
- Can you recommend a book or website that has helped you in your marriage?
- Whose example did you follow and what have you learned from your own mentors?
- Can you tell me about a time when you were on opposite pages but came to an agreement?
- When you come to an impasse, how do you make a decision as a unified couple?
- Were there times when you wanted to give up on your marriage? What did you do?
- What methods have you used to teach your kids about money?
- How do you manage your budget as a couple?
- What piece of advice would you give to a struggling couple?

Redefining Leadership: Brian

Movement from busy to prioritized requires focused leadership. Often, couples struggle with who should lead the charge in time and money management. The problem with leadership in marriage is not who leads but the definition of leadership itself. As a society, we receive mixed messages as to what defines leadership or what it should be. A common interpretation is that if you are a leader, you are in charge, the head honcho; you are in control.

Control is not leadership. Control is an illusion. Because of its elusive nature, the person attempting to assert dominion squeezes tighter in an effort to gain and maintain counterfeit power. The result manifests failure and the suffocation of trust. When control is the goal, your marriage cannot grow, will not succeed, and fails to be the best it can be.

The church often misses the mark on defining marital leadership. Well-intentioned pastors and theologians point to male headship in the marriage, but using this loaded term without an in-depth explanation and exegesis is dangerous. "Male headship" is an unclear phrase because "headship" otherwise escapes modern vernacular. Seriously, who says, "I'm the headship of the office" or "Johnny is a great city headship." When we use uncommon words like *headship*, we place too heavy a burden on the person interpreting those words. Lack of clarity is cruelty. When left up to interpretation, even well-meaning folks hear the word *head* and think "in charge." That trail leads back to the consequences of the goal of control.

The definition gets further jumbled and misunderstood when the church talks about stewardship in marriage. Stewardship is management. *You manage your finances; you don't manage your spouse.*

Pulling rank on your spouse tears at the fabric of your marriage. Don't mistake positional authority for leadership. Men, let me talk to you for just a second: you are not your wife's lord. You need to be leading without lording. She's already got a Lord. Be a leader. Real leaders sacrifice. Real leaders serve. Real leaders die to their own desires every day. This "others first" way of living establishes trust. It is easier to follow someone who you know is for you. Your job as a leader involves equipping your spouse to be the best person they can be. Your job requires you to build up and encourage your wife. This loving, sacrificing, trust-building, and equipping way of life leads your family well. If you and your wife do not lead your family, someone else will.

As to not leave you without practical tips on what sacrifice and service looks like, let's name a few. Protect your family's schedule. Begin removing nonessentials from your calendar. Schedule intentional time for the things that matter most, like praying for your spouse. Pick up the slack by taking on some of the routine household tasks your spouse usually handles. Choose spending time with your spouse over hobbies, clubs, rec leagues, or guys' or girls' night out. Go above and beyond to express your love to your spouse by how you order your days.

One of the best leadership questions you can ask yourself comes from Andy Stanley, author and pastor of North Point Community Church in Atlanta, Georgia: "What does love require of me?"[3] If you ask this question every day, you naturally steer yourself toward sacrifice and service. Follow Jesus. It is difficult to follow someone who can't make up their mind about which way they are headed. If you commit your life to learning and applying what it means to follow Christ, then you are going in the same direction. You always have the same constant. When your spouse follows your leadership, she moves toward a closer relationship with God because that's the direction you're going.

Breaking Up with Date Night: Cherie

Managing time and money well requires thinking differently. Sometimes the cherished ideals of others seep into what we think our finances and romance should look like. We need a new lens on old expectations and conventional wisdom. If we're to lead our lives well, we may even need to break with tradition.

Before we even began paying off debt, Brian and I broke up. We called it quits. We said not necessary, so long, sayonara. Let me explain.

In the early years of our marriage, a recurring piece of advice seemed to float around at many of our outings. In seminars, in small groups, during sermons, we repeatedly heard that in order to remain happily married, we needed one thing—regular date nights.

So we tried it. We put a date night on the calendar. At first we tried one per week. After realizing just how difficult it was to find childcare on a regular basis without bankrupting ourselves, we nixed that and settled on one date per month. But then life happened (oh, the busy!), we forgot to put it on the calendar one month, and we felt like we were awful human beings. With guilt in our guts and shame on our shoulders, we felt like our marriage just didn't measure up to those rock star once-a-week date nighters. They were destined for gold and platinum anniversaries while we were obviously doomed to divorce court.

And then we realized those notions were stupid. No date night, no matter how regular or how awesome, will make your marriage perfect. There's no magic formula that instantly adds intimacy to your relationship. If there was one, it's definitely not going to be found by eating expensive cheesecake, no matter how delicious.

We kissed date night goodbye.

Before you misunderstand me, I don't think date night is stupid. I don't think you're stupid if you have a date night. But I think that as a culture we've laid too many expectations at date night's door. We've unknowingly placed our hopes and dreams on one night a week dining out, while someone else watches our kids. We've depended on sitting silently in the theater, watching the latest blockbuster unfold, to fix our communication problems. Miniature golf, concerts, and shopping trips might provide a few moments of release from life's anxieties, but in the long run they don't help us discover deeper meaning or foster financial foreplay. Left unchecked, date night becomes more about where we're going or what we're doing instead of who we are with. We dangerously transfer what should be a time to connect into a temporary distraction.

Between work and the duties of home, the last thing you need is one more required activity. Does this mean you quit scheduling special time together? Of course not. Does it mean you are off the hook for regularly rekindling your romance? Not a chance.

However, thinking that date night waves the magic wand for all the problems in your marriage is a misnomer. In fact, oftentimes, regular date nights cause unforeseen problems, including financial problems. We may come to a planned evening out with unrealistic expectations. Too many rom coms set a blurry Hollywood standard on what date night is supposed to look like.

He'll be the perfect gentleman, suited up and arriving with a fresh cut flower. She'll be wearing a sexy red dress, with commercial coiffed hair and flawless makeup. They'll share a glass of wine at an upscale restaurant and chuckle over the day's events. After a five-star dinner, they'll hold hands while strolling along a canal and then finish the evening hot and sweaty, tangled in the sheets.

I don't know who these people are and how they got inside my head, but the date nights we've attempted pale in comparison. Usually Brian is still in his suit from work so that part's accurate. Everything else skews out of view because the nearest canal is thirty-five minutes away, we couldn't afford an upscale restaurant, and my naturally curly hair is always out of control (and usually in a ponytail).

Have you idealized date night, making it something it's not? It's time to shift your lens.

Spending time together looks different for every couple. When we were paying off $127,000 in debt, we didn't have the budget to afford a babysitter, let alone a fancy schmancy restaurant. We would have been happy to split a burger, but were making getting out of debt our first priority. Overspending on date night is not going to create harmony; instead, it causes money issues and marital discord.

When it comes to date night, seek the ordained in the ordinary. In the end, it doesn't really matter what you do, and reckless spending never equals a harmonious relationship. Instead of idealizing date night culture, try to carve out time in your regular schedule to connect. Every. Single. Night. This eliminates unrealistic expectations but raises the chances of actual connection.

Probably the easiest way to achieve this goal—especially if you have kids—is to commit to regular bedtimes for both you and your children. Intentionally set a specific time all of you will hit the hay and stick to it. Schedule the children's bedtime about an hour or more before yours (as your children age, this gets a bit more difficult, but it's not impossible). Use this time to connect. Share a snack. Play a game. Use the *Your Money, Your Marriage* online guide to have a money chat. Budget together. Hold hands in the quiet. Avoid the temptation to turn on the TV and zone out or scroll through countless feeds on your social media accounts.

This practice of "un-dating" both reduces your expenses (sitter + dinner + entertainment = big bucks) and also channels your quality time into a focused and purposeful experience. Plus, the pressure of one more date on the calendar disappears. You can relax and breathe together instead of feeling like you need to check another box or add another item on the to-do list. After all, spending time together shouldn't feel like a doctor's appointment or a parent-teacher conference.

There's only one requirement for each of your un-dates—a twenty-second hug. Scientific research continues to investigate and prove the health benefits of the practice of hugging. Hugs do all sorts of wonderful things for your body, including lowering blood pressure, reducing stress, and even healing wounds faster (how cool is that?). Studies also show regular and prolonged hugging creates a bond of trust between loving partners.[4] More than likely, twenty seconds of sustained hugging contact will do more to create a connection between you and your spouse than the fanciest of all date nights. And you gain the bonus of living longer too.

It's going to sound weird, but twenty seconds actually feels much longer than you think. The average hug lasts only three seconds.[5] But fight the feelings of discomfort and go deep for a great hug. It's difficult to be angry with anyone when you hug, and some of your differences might slip away. Plus, all you have to lose is twenty seconds of your time.

Let Mercy Lead

We both wore out a number of CDs when we were in college. For Brian, *Neil Diamond's Greatest Hits*, 2Pac's *All Eyez on Me*, and Garth

Brooks's *No Fences* ran on repeat. Cherie's list included Nirvana's *Nevermind*, Jewel's *Pieces of You*, dc Talk's *Jesus Freak*, and Rich Mullins's *Songs*. In one of the tracks from *Songs*, Mullins proclaims that we should "let mercy lead."

Mercy—not our calendars or our extracurriculars or our meetings or our volunteer opportunities—should guide our steps. Mercy should reign supreme in our households and our marriages. Mercy should prevail in every conversation we have about money. Moving from busy to prioritized requires leadership within marriage. Leadership fails without mercy.

True leadership doesn't derive influence from positional authority or a struggle for power or education. No, leadership in its truest essence is mercy. Wouldn't everyone's marriage flourish if it abounded with mercy? But we'll be the first to admit mercy isn't easy. And in a world where everyone seems to want a piece of our time and good opportunities overflow, we're likely to always struggle with busyness.

We've been in the same community group for over a decade. For ten years, we've met on Thursday nights at 6:30 p.m. While not always convenient, the commitment takes priority on our calendar. We know we grow in our faith and we grow closer together each time we show up. We know the people in our group expect us to love and cherish our marriage and manage our money well. We know if we stepped out of line, someone would lovingly intervene. Because of our shared value of community, Thursday nights are spoken for.

Early in our marriage, mentors of ours suggested if we had kids to only allow them to be involved in one sport at a time. This wise advice sheltered our young family as our girls grew up. No matter how amazing the opportunity, we took things one season at a time rather than double-booking our schedules. Our shared need for regular rest and moments of intimacy trumped extracurricular activities.

While we were paying off debt, we discovered that without weekly communication neither of us could possibly know the state of our finances. Regular conversations about income and upcoming expenses became indispensable. Our shared dream of living debt-free mandated intentional budget meetings.

As a couple, determine your values, needs, and dreams. By so doing, you lead your lives rather than letting life lead you. Prioritized time and money management provides the space you need on your calendar for you and your spouse to connect. And by connect, we mean on every level . . . the talking sort and the winky, nontalking sort.

Discussion Questions

1. Do you feel too busy? What tools and strategies do you use to help combat the pull of the busy cycle?
2. Brian said, "Margin in our lives safeguards sanctity in the sheets." How can busyness and lack of margin kill intimacy in marriages?
3. Cherie, quoting Mr. Kalugyer, said, "I don't care how good you are. You have to take direction from someone." Do you have a money mentor? If you could ask a happily married couple one question about money, intimacy, and marriage, what would it be?
4. Brainstorm a short list of couples you may want to approach to be a money mentor. What qualifies those couples to speak into your life?
5. Brian said, "If you do not lead your family, someone

else will." When have you found this to be true in your own household? Your upbringing? In the lives of friends or acquaintances?

6. Have you ever over-romanticized date night? What happened when your expectations went unmet?

Fostering Financial Foreplay

- Craft a creative date night of your own. Make it an "un-date" by planning the details together and spending as little money as possible. Whether it's a walk around the neighborhood holding hands or time spent on the couch together dreaming big about your future, keep the plan simple and meaningful.
- Try the Twenty-Second-Hug Experiment. For one week, hug your spouse each day for at least twenty seconds. If you want to, record your fully clothed hug (seriously, people, keep it clean) and upload it to YouTube or Instagram using the #YourMoneyYourMarriage hashtag. Share how hugging for a prolonged period made you feel.

CHAPTER 6

Who's the Boss?

From Control to Trust

The best way to find out if you can trust somebody is to trust them.

ERNEST HEMINGWAY

Our daughter Zoe loves field day. She loves the competition, the end-of-the-year frenzy, and, of course, winning. She loves the obstacle courses, the foot races, the popsicles, and the crowning event of any field day experience—a tug-of-war contest between the girls and boys. With great anticipation, we sent her off to end third grade on the best day of the year. Covered in sunblock and armed with a bottle of water bearing her name, she grinned from ear to ear.

We knew when she returned home she'd tell the finest (and longest) tales of the day and give us 150 reasons why this was her one shining moment, her highest achievement, and the most storied day of her nine-year existence. This is why we were both shocked when she climbed off the school bus that afternoon and burst into tears as soon as her feet touched the driveway, declaring, "Worst! Field Day! Ever!"

A quick look at her face justified her dramatic reaction. A large purple lump swelled under one eye. From the base of her neck all the way up to her left ear prickled a long, wide, red abrasion. She looked like she had thrown down in a dark alley instead of attending the neighborhood elementary school. As we began breaking down the day's events, trying to get to the bottom of it all, while also determining if she needed further medical attention, the pieces came together.

The soon-to-be black eye was an accidental injury inflicted by the gate of the kickball field. But the scrape on her neck—a rope burn—precipitated from her favorite event: the tug of war. It seemed that while the girls had prevailed at pulling the flag over the line to score the win, this left the boys angered with the result. Frustrated (and probably embarrassed), the entire lot of fellas continued pulling in the opposite direction after the ladies let down their guards. The outcome landed Zoe on the ground with a large, thick rope running over her neck. Ouch.

It was a battle of the sexes, a struggle for power and control. The pushing and pulling handed one team bruised egos and at least one of the participants on the other side a physical injury that would take weeks to heal. Our inner mama and papa bears wanted to show up at lunchtime the next day and line out each and every one of the boys responsible for not only hurting our baby girl's neck but also for spoiling her favorite day of the year. Someone needed to teach them a quintessential life lesson: When you lose a game of tug-of-war, you put down the rope.

Moving from control to trust in our marriages, especially when it comes to hot topics like sex and money, might look more like a third-grade tug-of-war than we'd care to admit. Maybe it's because both of us want to make all the decisions. Maybe it's because we like the idea of being in charge. Maybe it's because we'd both like to be the center of attention. Or maybe it's simply because no one ever modeled a healthy picture of what it looks like to trust each other. The struggle is real; we yank back and forth on the rope of our relationship, pushing and pulling to get our own way. All the while, we wildly wield power, recklessly disregarding the damaging effects to the other person. When married couples lay down the urge to control one another, they move to a place of trust. While perhaps easier said than done, concrete strategies do exist to help you and your spouse begin to trust each other and to finally drop the rope.

The One about Lilacs, Wiggly Teeth, and Judith Light: Brian

My three biggest fears in reverse order are: lilacs, wiggly teeth, and Judith Light. Long ago, seasonal allergies afflicted me with a lifetime of misery and consternation, so I can rationalize my fight-or-flight response to the otherwise innocuous purple spring flowers. While more difficult to explain the reason, wiggly teeth make me woozy, and everything gets fuzzy like I'm about to have a sitcom flashback.

Prior to marriage, and well before children, this irrational fear led me to make a completely one-sided deal: Cherie handles the wiggly teeth, and I clean up the sickness of our children. To date, Cherie has not pulled one tooth. In her shrewdness, she taught the children to pull their own teeth. We have two kids. I've cleaned and sanitized the aftermath of many stomach bugs. The number of teeth a kid has is finite, but the number of times a kid gets sick is immeasurable. Regardless, I still consider it to be the Best. Deal. Ever. I don't want to see your wiggly tooth. Somehow blood, head injuries, an arm broken in three places, and all the other gross things that go along with parenting don't affect me. Everybody has their thing, I guess.

If my self-diagnosed honondasdontiaphobia (fear of losing teeth) sounds a little wacky, then my unwarranted fear of 1980s sitcom star Judith Light must seem cuckoo for Cocoa Puffs. Look, I'm sure she's a wonderful human being. But if there happens to be a rerun of her hit series *Who's the Boss?* on, I dive for the remote like I'm protecting a platoon from a live grenade—even if it's not my remote. Want me to give up national secrets? Save yourself the trouble of torturing me and just put on one episode of *Who's the Boss?*, because I'll spill my guts before the first commercial break.

Upon honest reflection, I realized Judith Light was not my true fear. Usually, I excused my discomfort by blaming her Dallas Cowboys-sized shoulder pads. But at its core, my genuine disdain originates from somewhere other than horrific 80s fashion. A struggle entrenched deep in my heart is the controversy of who is in charge. Remember, the premise of the show centers around this tension. Was it Judith Light's character, Angela—a career-oriented advertising executive? Or was it Tony Danza's character, Tony—a retired baseball player turned housekeeper? Tony and Angela weren't married, but if unaddressed, the same strife increases until it fractures our own relationships. Who is in charge (or who's the boss?) in your marriage proves a critical question. The Bible sheds light on this ancient query:

> Submit to one another out of reverence for Christ. Wives, submit yourselves to your own husbands as you do to the Lord.

> For the husband is the head of the wife as Christ is the head of the church, his body, of which he is the Savior. Now as the church submits to Christ, so also wives should submit to their husbands in everything.
>
> Husbands, love your wives, just as Christ loved the church and gave himself up for her to make her holy, cleansing her by the washing with water through the word, and to present her to himself as a radiant church, without stain or wrinkle or any other blemish, but holy and blameless.
>
> **EPHESIANS 5:21–27**

Maybe we're asking the wrong question when we ask, "Who's the boss?" Maybe the better question is, "Who's guiding our money and our marriage?" When reading Ephesians 5, sometimes the reader only sees the word *submission*. Bible closed. All done—don't want to hear that. But before you push back, if God is one of your shared values, the Bible helps resolve these complicated issues and alleviate conflict.

Your shared values guide everything in your marriage.

Take a look at verse 21: "Submit to one another out of reverence for Christ." Submission is supposed to be mutual. More important, mutual submission rises from reverence to one person: Jesus. When you submit to your spouse, you are submitting to Christ Himself. Do not confuse submission with subjugation. One spouse lording power over the other contradicts God's plan. Mutual submission honors God and reminds us that everything belongs to Him. Your money. Your marriage. Your life. Being entrusted with great gifts does not convey ownership over anything. Caring for and tending to your money, marriage, and life is a biblical mandate. Recognizing mutual submission as a guiding value and truth in your life can launch your journey toward relinquishing control.

Once couples abandon the quest for control, they preserve and maximize trust. Wise people build great marriages on a foundation of trust because trust leads to intimacy. Old wounds heal and battle scars fade into distant memory when we stop grasping for something as illusory as control. Controlling financial behaviors, and even worse, controlling bedroom behaviors will crack otherwise firm foundations. Spouses discover peace instead of conflict when the unrealistic and unwinnable struggle for control ceases.

In the end, married couples are not ranked by who's the breadwinner or who's more domestically inclined. *Marriage is not a competition. It's a collaboration.* Angela needed Tony and Tony needed Angela (truthfully, Angela needed Tony to take his seam ripper to those shoulder pads, amiright?). You need your wife. You need your husband. You make each other better and can accomplish dreams beyond comprehension by resting in your interdependence instead of fighting for dominance.

Money, Sex, Vulnerability, and Powerlessness: Cherie

I absolutely hate throwing up. I have sympathy gag reflex, and, hence, before Brian and I decided to marry, I brokered what I consider to be my best economical move of all time. He cleans up any of the girls' ick, and I aid and assist when it comes to wiggly teeth. I'm not really bothered by wiggly teeth, so I considered this to be a killer deal. Plus, as I conveyed to Brian, if I attempt to clean things up, I'm probably going to get sick to my stomach, so he would be managing twice the mess anyway.

My brilliance (read: dumb luck) played out as the years passed. Our first child successfully removed all of her own baby chompers.

The second child pulled the majority of her set too. Only a year or two left to go and my end of the bargain has played out well. Brian's responsibilities will probably endure at least another decade. #winning

Let's return to my own personal issues with tummy troubles. Honestly, it grosses me out even typing the words or thinking about the whole process. True story: if I read on Facebook that someone in your family caught a bug, I go immediately to the sink and wash my hands. However, my issues probably have nothing to do with the physicality of the act but stem from my own struggles with control.

(Insert Janet Jackson musical interlude.)

I'm afraid of losing control. I'm afraid of being powerless. I'm afraid of being subjugated, bossed around, or limited.

But marriage (if it's to be successful) routinely requires each of us to lay down the control, to put aside our own wants, expectations, desires, and longings. It necessitates an attitude of "you first" and "What can I do to help, no matter what it costs me?"

Perhaps when we first walked the aisle, we romanticized that—of course we will both willingly place the needs of our spouse over our own. I mean, after all, we're in love. Who wouldn't want to do that? However, when the rubber meets the road, love in action is much more challenging. You probably figured out this simple truth, say, within the first week (or first few days) of marriage.

Before we go too much further, I want to make a clear statement about what I *don't* mean. Laying aside your control is not the same thing as subjecting yourself to abuse. If your spouse attacks you with physical violence, manipulatively withholds or mandates sex, uses derogatory language, or excludes you from any of your household finances, your relationship needs professional counseling. If your safety (or the safety of your children) is at risk, you need to seek shelter immediately and contact the authorities. You are loved and precious. Please ask for help.[1]

My lifelong struggle with the ideas of marriage and control originated in a small, dusty Sunday school classroom of a Thomas Kinkade-styled church in rural Indiana during my middle school years. Each week my friend (the only other class participant) and I sat in folding chairs, trying not to doze off, while the pastor's wife drilled us with questions.

In the instructor's mind, these questions had succinct and specific answers. We were not allowed to ask further questions in response. One week when we did, she prayed God would heal our "contentious" hearts. Once we got home and looked up the word *contentious* in the dictionary (pre-Siri days, here), we were pretty ticked off.

On one Sunday in particular, she explained marriage in the faith context. She began to talk about fearing your husband. In my head several pubescent questions began to knock around. I dared not ask them out loud though. My friend, who was always a bit bolder than me (and maybe more contentious), did ask a follow up.

"Hold on, wait. We're supposed to be scared of our future husbands? That doesn't sound right."

The pastor's wife said, "Well, not like you're scared of a horror movie. But, you know, just like you really want to please him. For instance, when you bake him your first pie, you're afraid of whether or not he'll like it."

(P.S. Welcome to my fractured psyche. It's a little scary in here, and I'm still trying to figure it out.) This was a confusing and semi-terrifying message for eleven-year-old me to receive. I had no idea how to even bake a pie or that Brian (who I wouldn't meet for more than a decade) would require me to make pies. And, oh crap, now I have to be scared of both my future husband *and* baking pies?

As my armpits began to sweat and my stomach churned, the idea of marriage began to seem unnecessary. Who wants to spend their entire life in fear? Of course I packed these insecurities, misgivings, and confused thoughts neatly into my own psychological and spiritual baggage and promptly forgot about them. Fast forward ten or eleven years, and I had carried those ideas straight down the aisle and right along on our honeymoon. Within a year or two, I began to realize my complete rejection of the pastor's wife's ideas had caused a vicious overcorrect, where I now longed to be the center of my own marriage.

I wanted to call the shots. Maybe not when it came to the choices Brian made, but certainly when it came to determining my own financial options. And by now you know this type of thinking on both of our parts yielded a massive amount of debt. When you buy whatever you want to buy, whenever you want to buy it, and your spouse does the same thing, you end up spending more than you make. When you detest the idea of a budget because it controls what you can and can't do, you miss the mark for a secure financial future every single time. The illusion of being in control leads to the exact opposite when it comes to your money and your marriage. You wind up with your finances and relationship careening out of control.

All of this is to say that the idea of yielding control makes me afraid. But let's get one thing straight. Pie is never to be feared, only savored and devoured. However, I typically buy pie because my baking prowess never developed, even after the admonitions of my adolescent years.

The fear of yielding control plagues so many of us as we pursue our happily ever afters. Whether we stand naked before our spouses or we open up our wallets to share our receipts, we fear not just a loss of control but judgment too. In the bedroom, each of our imperfections are clearly on display—every wrinkle, every blemish, every bit of our misshapen torsos—all become apparent, blatantly visible to our husband or wife. In the same way, when we open up our checkbooks and financial lives, every mistake—each impulse-buy and clear, concrete evidence of precisely how we've blown it with our money—is all laid bare.

This is truly frightening.

It also presents an invitation. A great deal of marriage revolves around learning how to become vulnerable with one another in the midst of our imperfections. It's a delicate dance filled with terrific tension. Perhaps deep in our souls we question if anyone could truly love us if they knew how deeply flawed we really are. Can we completely entrust our blemished bodies and our money mistakes to our spouses? Can we give up control and build a relationship where we let go of the reins of power? Can we truly trust our partners?

Doing so never comes without risk or the crippling fear of being naked and exposed before someone. Author Alain de Botton speaks into these fears and that great risk of marriage with the following words, "Marriage ends up as a hopeful, generous, infinitely kind gamble taken by two people who don't know yet who they are or who the other might be, binding themselves to a future they cannot conceive of and have carefully avoided investigating."[2]

Rather than terror, we turn to hope. Yes, each of us is "less than" in so many ways. We blow it and miss the mark every day (please tell me I'm not alone here). However, when we begin to expose our mistakes to our husbands or wives with a spirit of humility, we dare to gamble on trust. We dare to allow ourselves to be vulnerable, and we begin to grasp that perhaps we can be loved while stripped bare, imperfections and all.

Recently, I listened to a podcast where a Franciscan monk explored a theology of vulnerability. He reflected on how many of the prayers of the Christian faith begin with the words *almighty God*. Truly, most believers assent that God is almighty, the Creator of the universe, the One who hung the stars, all while pouring out great love on them. However, the monk went on to proclaim the truth that God is equally vulnerable.[3]

The very incarnation of Jesus exemplifies the vulnerability of God. He came to earth in the form of a defenseless infant. Rather than charge through the skies, riding on a thunderbolt, He was formed within the womb, a mixture of tiny capillaries and tender skin. Yes, He is almighty God, but He is also all-vulnerable God. And perhaps He understands a bit more of the fear of being naked before someone else than we give Him credit for.

Your act of relinquishing control within marriage and moving toward trust is an act of worship. When you choose to present yourself fully to your spouse, you foster financial foreplay, dropping fearful barriers to draw nearer to one another in a state of trusting openness when it comes both to money and intimacy. But much more than that, you reenact a Christlikeness marked on your soul. You reflect the very nature of God in your choices.

Releasing the tight grip we've placed on our money waxes and wanes in its moments of challenge and ease. Giving things over to God, over time, becomes more natural, but for me it never becomes easier. I regularly have to pry my white-knuckled fingers off the areas of life I find difficult to yield. But it's never a hopeless pursuit. When I give up the illusion of being able to control my marriage or life, I usually become aware of the great release and freedom my actions bring. Letting go—moving from control to trust—makes me feel fully alive.

When I'm willing to let go of my need for control, my eyes open to new possibilities. My marriage blossoms with the fruit of trust. When it comes to money, I'm less likely to think Brian is out to get me and instead begin to grasp a vision of us working together toward common financial goals. The foundation we build together in trust when it comes to our shared finances results in a deeper physical connection too. Instead of viewing amorous approaches as his attempts to gain something from me, I begin to understand our vulnerable physical interactions with one another lend me the opportunity to build an even greater trust within our marriage.

The $1,300 Parking Fee: Brian

Upon exiting the parking garage, I swiped my debit card through the self-pay machine, the cross-arm lifted, and I slammed the accelerator. As I raced to a meeting thirty minutes away, it occurred to me that something was amiss. With my eyes fixed on the proper route back to my office, I had failed to observe the exorbitant parking cost. The receipt caught my attention at a stoplight, and I exclaimed, "Three hundred dollars!" At the next stoplight, I managed to call the telephone number on the receipt. By the grace of God, the parking company's manager, Sheila, answered the phone, which, she later informed me, she rarely does. Out of kindness, Sheila reviewed a list of transactions from the garage I exited and assured me there had been no three-hundred-dollar charge. My relief fleeted as she declared, "Aw, honey, it's worse than that. You spent $1,300. Our machines can't print that many digits on a receipt so it must have dropped the 1."

"What? I only parked for two hours!" Because Sheila was the nicest parking garage manager in the profession's history, she agreed to take a look at the receipt once I could send it to her.

Even though I was pressed for time, with back-to-back meetings and the need to email my new BFF, Sheila, my attention shifted to our finances. *Thirteen hundred dollars will really mess up the checking account if I don't do something quick*, I thought. Our budget did not include paying $1,300 for parking in a downtown garage. But I was driving, and you shouldn't bank and drive. So I called Cherie. "I need you to transfer some money into the checking account. I just spent $1,300 on parking." While this was strange to say, I'm sure it was even more bizarre to hear. My circumstances limited my options and forced me to get right to the point. Those two sentences were all I said to Cherie before ending the call.

After a few unsuccessful attempts to scan and email the receipt to Sheila, I finally forwarded a picture of it. Sheila canceled the excessive charge. It turns out that a few months earlier I had stayed at a hotel where, upon entrance, the parking garage issued me a ticket similar to the one from Sheila's garage. However, guests exited the parking garage using their room keys. Being a creature of habit, I placed Sheila's ticket in the exact spot of the hotel ticket. When reaching for my ticket to exit Sheila's garage, I grabbed the hotel ticket. The machine at Sheila's garage read the magnetic code on the hotel ticket and charged me for three months' worth of parking. Sheila removed the $1,300 charge and comped my parking because the machine from her garage should not have read the code from another garage. What a relief and great customer service.

I arrived home hours later, forgetting all about the $1,300 parking charge from earlier that day. Cherie, on the other hand, remembered. She asked, "So why did I have to transfer $1,300?" I immediately apologized for not calling her after its resolution and explained what happened. We confirmed the voided transaction and transferred $1,300 back to our savings account. That was the sum total of the discussion between Cherie and me.

Aside from a complicated scheme to gain free downtown

parking, we learned two important lessons from the fiasco. First, having $1,300 can prevent financial disaster. Years of frugality, toil, and paying off debt got us to the point where my $1,300 error would not have broken us. A few years prior, an unexpected $1,300 hit would have overdrawn our funds and bounced a litany of checks. I'm confident my conversation with Sheila wouldn't have succeeded either, let alone my conversation with Cherie. *Financial stress inhibits effective communication.*

The second and more powerful lesson gained: trust takes time. Cherie trusted me enough to know that if I made a confounding request, it must be legitimate—embarrassing, but legitimate. Unwavering trust doesn't happen overnight. Since I had not made multiple strange and excessive financial requests over the course of our marriage, Cherie trusted me without hesitation in a critical time-constrained moment. She wasn't harsh, she didn't freak out, she didn't even call later to ask, "You did what?" In order to achieve a higher level of trust with your finances and beyond, employ the following habits.

Be consistent. Let your yes be yes and your no be no. Consistency fosters financial foreplay. Why? *Because following through on your word is sexy.* When you make any kind of promise and fulfill it to your spouse, the balance in your "trust account" goes up. Following through on your financial commitments yields trust in all areas of your marriage, including the bedroom. It's easier to make a promise than to keep a promise. Couples who agree on a financial plan and adhere to the plan know they can trust one another. Cherie trusted me in my parking garage gaffe because I'm consistent in my frugality and refrain from goofball financial moves. Cherie built trust with me by not overreacting about my financial error and inattention.

A vow is a vow. Committing to your financial plan isn't about the five, ten, or one hundred dollars spent or saved but about a sacred promise. In marriage, all promises are sacred. When you agree on your finances and follow through, the commitment communicates a message without words: "She's serious about this" or "He's really going to keep his promises." The message translates even deeper because establishing trust in your finances constructs confidence in your vows. "He does what he says he's going to do" transcends finances. If you can handle the little things, you can handle the big things. It might seem silly that fulfilling a small pledge like "I'm not going to grab my morning latte" for just a couple of weeks evidences commitment not only to the budget but also to your mate.

Earning trust by attending to details harkens a biblical precept. Consider these words from Luke 16:10–13: "Whoever can be trusted with very little can also be trusted with much, and whoever is dishonest with very little will also be dishonest with much. So if you have not been trustworthy in handling worldly wealth, who will trust you with true riches? And if you have not been trustworthy with someone else's property, who will give you property of your own? 'No one can serve two masters. Either you will hate the one and love the other, or you will be devoted to the one and despise the other. You cannot serve both God and money.'"

Start small. Go big or go home is not the answer here. *The steady steps of small decisions over time pave the path to the pinnacle of trust.* If you go too big, too fast, you will fail with a capital *F.* For example, instead of just giving up your morning latte habit, you decide to give up coffee, caffeine, sugar, sugar substitutes, meat, social media, cable TV, video games, and all your annoying habits (oh, you have them). I'll play the odds on this one, and take the sure bet you're going to fail—miserably. When you declare lofty intentions to your spouse and fall short within the hour, it takes longer than you realize to rebound. However, if you start with attainable goals and persist over time, your spouse notices more successes than failures. Through dependability and fortitude, you slowly release control and steadily build trust.

No money secrets. Nothing breaches financial trust faster than discovering money secrets. Secrets destroy household finances and crush intimacy. Keeping secrets about money leads to keeping secrets about extramarital affairs. Cheating on your spouse starts somewhere. Keeping secrets with money trains you to lie to your husband or wife for selfish pursuits. It's financial infidelity. Financial infidelity is a close look-a-like cousin to marital infidelity. They have the same last name. Initially, you'll get away with lying and the secret will feel safe. Eventually, the habitual secret-keeping grows and festers into your entire relationship. Secrecy in finances can take the form of: "I like to have a secret stash of cash so he doesn't know what I bought" or "I have a checking account in just my name because he/she can't manage money" or the extreme "Hopefully she doesn't know about my one-hundred-thousand-dollar credit card debt I racked up from gambling online." If it's the smaller version, quit. If it's toward the larger side of a financial secret, put down this book immediately and call your pastor or a counselor to help walk you through what to do to come clean.

Pedaling Forward: Cherie

For my fortieth birthday, Brian bought me the deepest desire of my heart—a vintage-style Huffy cruiser bicycle. My sweet, canary-yellow ride came completely tricked out with a large basket on the front, a cup holder made just for the mile and a half ride to Starbucks, and a separate compartment perfectly sized for my iPhone—the music could stream out of the speakers as I pedaled down the street. I quickly secured myself an adorable helmet so I could cruise around the neighborhood and back and forth to the gym. I could not have been happier. Until I actually sat on the bike for the first time.

I forgot that the last time I rode a bike without handbrakes I was approximately age ten. I love cycling. But three decades of braking without using your feet is a difficult habit to break, and, believe it or not, things didn't come back to me "just like riding a bike." Terrified, I envisioned myself unable to come to a complete stop and skidding into oncoming traffic. In a brief moment of panic, I contemplated telling Brian I couldn't possibly ride the long-sought-after object of my affection. He would need to immediately return it from whence it came.

Standing at the end of the driveway with my heart pounding and my bike balanced between my legs, I knew I had a decision to make. I could put my feet on the pedals and move forward, or I could turn around and park the bike in our garage. Parking the bike was my safest choice. After all, if I didn't ride it, I wouldn't be able to skin my knees or plow down an angry goose in a failed attempt at braking. But in that moment, I began to think of all I would miss if I chose the more conservative option: no wind in my face, no endorphin high from coasting down the hill, no extra burned calories, allowing me to indulge in an ice cream cone on a hot day. My choice paralysis ebbed and flowed between the known and unknown, preservation and adventure. What felt like hours passed until the first track on my playlist concluded, and I knew I needed to do something.

And so, with little fanfare, I pushed off and pedaled down the street. More than once I caught myself reverting to old habits, squeezing invisible levers in an attempt to slow down. Afraid I'd lose my balance when standing up to pedal, I pushed through a seated climb and spiked my heart rate even higher. That first ride left me sweaty and with numb hands from holding the handlebars in a viselike grip. But I did it. And ride after ride, I began to get the feel for that new bike. While my fears haven't completely vanished, the inner dialogue before I take off lasts only a few seconds instead of an entire song.

In the same way riding my yellow Huffy caused me to become paralyzed with doubt and fear, marriages can gridlock after financial and sexual infidelity. The consequences leave us debating at the end of a metaphorical marriage driveway. Can we trust again? Should we simply park our relationship and leave things status quo? Does the risk of the ride outweigh the potential payoff? They're not simple questions to answer and traveling through them will require much more time than a single track on a playlist.

I won't pretend Brian and I have struggled with the exact same issues you and your spouse have. But we've witnessed some of our closest friends experience the sting of broken promises and sexual infidelity. We know couples who battled the pain of one spouse making major purchases (read: at one point, a ridiculously expensive vehicle) without the knowledge of the other. Broken trust cracks each and every marriage vow, causing us to question if we can rely on anything ever promised. The pain of each tiny fracture splinters in a million directions, fragmenting our hearts and causing division.

Remember, financial foreplay requires movement. We can't merely hope and wish for the best. We can't remain static, frozen in the drive. We have to pedal. We must move forward. We have to pick up the pieces, glue them back together, praying for a mosaic instead of a mess. Yes, our old, tired habits will likely creep into our brains and the rhythms of our movements. But over time, we can learn to begin to trust our husbands and wives and the promises we've made to one another.

The jury's out on whether or not I'll quit it with my inner bike-fear dialogue before I take off down the street. It may be a lifelong conflict between my head and my heart. But I do know that each time I take the risk to trust, fear loses a little. And the payoff of taking a chance far outweighs the potential for disaster. No, I can't control my lovely yellow bike or my marriage. But I can enjoy the ride.

Release the Rope

Just like Zoe with her field day rope burns, we may have been injured by a spouse struggling for control. We overdraw the account. We take over the finances and checkbook with a hostile attitude. We make major purchases without discussion. We run up a credit card in secret. If our spouse discovered the truth, the intimacy and trust in our relationships diminished. If he or she still doesn't know, we painfully cower in shame, dreading an unveiling of our financial transgressions.

However, our stories don't have to end there. We must choose to lay down the rope and begin building a relationship built on trusting each other instead of trying to control one another. Remaining in the same unhealthy patterns yields the same unhealthy results. Over and over again, we chase one another in an attempt to exert our power and get our way. An ugly cycle of control develops with no true winners. At best, we cling to our end of the rope, pulling and bearing down, immovable in the fight. At worst, one of us lies wounded on the ground with the rope running over his or her neck.

It's time to put down the rope so we can . . .

- rethink our definition of submission.
- realize the only behaviors we can control are our own.
- recognize our need for vulnerability and how being vulnerable reflects Jesus's love for us.
- risk taking our husbands or wives at their word, even if we've been burned before.

Losing control invokes fear. Trusting your spouse requires courage. You foster financial foreplay when you choose trust over control, courage over fear.

Discussion Questions

1. Do you have any odd or funny fears like Brian's fears of wiggly teeth and Judith Light?
2. "Mutual submission honors God and reminds us that everything belongs to Him." How does recognizing that everything—especially our money and our marriages—belongs to God change your perspective on who's the boss?
3. With your spouse, discuss what healthy vulnerability looks like in the context of your marriage. Then name instances when you have felt vulnerable in the bedroom. In a small-group setting, describe vulnerable money moments in your marriage.
4. What's the most you've ever paid for parking? How would you have reacted to Brian's $1,300 parking charge? Roleplay the phone call scenario with your

spouse. Pretend to call your husband or wife on the phone and say, "I need you to transfer $1,300 into checking" and see where it goes. Then reverse roles.

5. Describe your first bicycle. When have you chosen to take a risk even though you were afraid? What was the result?

Fostering Financial Foreplay

- It's time to get honest. Share any financial secret, struggle, or temptation you've been keeping from your spouse. After you've both had time to disclose your imperfections, pray together, asking God to help you move from control to trust. If necessary, schedule an appointment with your pastor, a financial counselor, or a marriage counselor to help you work through those challenging issues.
- Trust Talk: Someone rear-ends you on your way home from work. Your son or daughter falls off the monkey bars and breaks an arm. Your water heater leaks everywhere and needs to be replaced. What would you do in unexpected stressful financial circumstances? Discuss and determine your plan of action in case of disaster.

CHAPTER 7

Where's That At Again?

From Scattered to Organized

A good system shortens the road to the goal.

ORISON SWETT MARDEN

For the first three years of our marriage, we served as a local church's youth directors. Parents entrusted their teenagers to our care, instruction, and wisdom, apparently not noticing we were only about five years older than most of the students. We routinely invited the teens into our home—a modest two-bedroom, one bath, second floor, outdoor walk-up apartment built circa 1975. We had no idea just how sketchy the complex was until a parent asked for the address and looked quasi-horrified at our response.

The first nine months of married life tests any couple. Since we married at a young age, the learning curve was steep. We learned how to cook and clean our own space without a parent or RA checking our work. We balanced grad school, jobs, and ministry together for the first time. Grocery shopping, laundry, bill payment, and automobile maintenance all became our joint responsibility. The challenges of merging finances, household organization, and twenty-two years' worth of patterned behaviors (both good and bad) met us within those incredibly thin walls of our first tiny apartment. By the way, we're still not sure why those parents were so worried. It was a safe neighborhood. The police visited the complex almost every single night.

We'd love to tell you about how we aced that honeymoon experience, how every detail of our new relationship came together without a hiccup. However, we're sure you're guessing that might be a complete and total lie, which it would be. There are plenty of accurate phrases and words to describe those first few months of marital bliss—happy and sweet, innocent and teeming with life. Also? Hot mess. A big, stinking hot mess in every sense possible, but mostly manifested in regard to our physical space.

Our small apartment always seemed to overflow with dirty everything—dirty laundry, dirty dishes, dirty shoes, dirty counters. The outward clutter reflected the state of our checkbook too. With no budget or financial goals, a flutter of receipts clouded around us worse than Pig-Pen's cloud of dust in *Peanuts*. The mess took a toll on our sex lives too. One winter night, our slothfulness resulted in sleeping on our lumpy, "springs poking you in the back" sleeper sofa mattress because we were too lazy to put away the clean laundry on our bed. Let's just say an uncomfortable reclining position and blaming each other for the mess didn't lead to a hot night of passion.

Like small children who refuse to put away their toys, we were setting in motion practices and systems that would take years to undo. Through our failures, we began to identify a need to change our behaviors to keep us from falling into the black hole of our own mess. While you're unlikely to see our present-day home displayed on an organizational website, we've placed a priority on moving from a scattered mess to an organized process in both our home and our finances.

Inundated with too much stuff, our culture floods with excess. And financial clutter leads to bigger problems than an overflowing closet. Being scattered with your stuff makes it more difficult to be connected in your marriage. And if your life is a mess, chances are you won't hop into bed each night readied for romance. You see, our exterior lives and our interior lives are closely related. And if our physical space is a mess, chances are our internal state will start to feel like a mess too. Financial foreplay requires moving from a state of being scattered to a realm of organization. Envision setting the mood for romance; most likely you don't toss garbage everywhere. Fostering true intimacy for your money and your marriage springs from a place of order and peace, not chaos.

Philosophical changes and even heart changes are a good start, but they aren't enough. When couples transition toward organizing their homes and finances, their relationship becomes more fulfilling.

Declutter Your Money: Brian

During my senior year of college, I arrived home and found my roommate outside, laughing at a utility worker's misfortune. Strange events often occurred around that midcentury bungalow rental, so my roommate mocking a man in a hard hat, while cruel, was par for the course. Declining to heckle another human, I inquired what was so funny. It turns out the man was from the water company and had struggled with opening the access to our home's water main. He applied too much torque, broke his tool, and ruined his effort. The joke was lost on me. My roommate found it humorous because the water company's employee attempted to disconnect our water and failed. While he found the situation hilarious, the fact that our water bill went unpaid infuriated me.

My roommate held the responsibility of paying certain bills. I paid him my share every month and he cut the check to the utility . . . or at least he was supposed to. Apparently, in his confounding system, he retrieved the mail before me and placed the bills in a kitchen drawer. He confessed that after the bills were in the drawer, he ignored them. My payment toward the bills also disappeared into the drawer along with his contribution. He wasn't embezzling or even in dire straits financially; he was just really sloppy. When my roommate opened the bill drawer, envelopes, cash, and statements rained onto the kitchen floor. Other than setting the bills on fire, it's tough to imagine a more ridiculous method of financial management. His scattered system, while ladened with the best intentions, was doomed to fail.

A cluttered financial system (or no system at all) hijacks your financial future. Hopefully you don't have a neglected drawer flooded with unpaid, overdue bills. Even the best maintained household finances benefit from periodic decluttering. If you have incurred interest fees on credit cards, late fees on any bills, ATM fees, overdraft fees, or if you have overspent, made an impulse purchase, panicked because you forgot a bill was due, or been human, decluttering can prevent money problems.

However, decluttering can tempt you to start cleaning your whole house. Mired down in the job, you overlook the most essential piece of the puzzle—the budget. I get it; physical decluttering yields a visible impact as opposed to intangible budgeting. But, like an invisible carbon monoxide leak, the lack of a budget kills unsuspecting couples. Your household's budget serves as a sealant to prevent money from leaking out of your hands and sounds an alarm if it detects something wrong.

We suggest you make the budget as physical as possible. When you put pen to paper, your brain is more likely to remember the experience.[1] Remembering your budget will help you stick to its guidelines. Writing down your financial plan also makes it feel more real than an abstract spreadsheet. Going analog with your budget also eliminates distractions. The inbox doesn't ping, no notifications for cat videos pop up, and you're not tempted to scroll through photos of your cousin's new baby. This process even puts you and your spouse literally on the same page at the same time. Choose to place your analog budget in a specific binder or folder in an agreed upon designated space in your home. Fight the temptation to just leave your plan out on the kitchen table or to stuff it into a desk drawer. This little personal finance treasure map guides your family's future. Treat it with care.

Together, and naked if possible (because everything is better when you're naked), write down your income at the top of the page and categorize your giving, saving, and spending. For a full guide on how to set percentages for giving, saving, and spending, consult the *Your Money, Your Marriage* online guide. Spoiler: giving and saving or paying off debt should come before spending.[2] While not mandatory, naked budget meetings lower your defenses and make the practice more fun. If you opt for a clothes-on session, make time to make out after you've completed the task. But back to the basics: list everything you plan to spend at the beginning of the month and agree to the plan. Effective budgeting requires spending less than your combined income. Balanced checkbooks are sexy. Establishing your household finances together leads to trust.[3] Disclosure, mutual agreement, and a shared, written plan create confidence. According to a recent *Money* survey, "couples who trust their partner with finances felt more secure, argued less, and had more fulfilling sex lives."[4]

Budgets embody sacred promises that promote our values, provide for our needs, and help us reach our shared dreams. After years of assisting people with their financial lives, I recently learned a simple truth that blew my mind. This is life-changing stuff. *The word* budget *contains . . . wait for it . . . the word* budge. Part of having a budget means you have to budge. Your spouse has to budge, but so do you. Both of you must participate in the process and suggest and make changes.

Once you've agreed to the spending plan, create a system that works for you both. Because couples are wired differently, your organizational system—whether paper budget forms, budgeting software like Quicken, or an app like Mint—may not work for your spouse. *You're not married to your system; you're married to your spouse.* Make like Elsa and let it go. Selfishly clinging to a system that only works for you alienates your spouse from financial matters. Ultimately, forcing your spouse into a foreign methodology proves counterproductive. Financial foreplay is about being in rhythm with marital money and intimacy. Diverging from a unified fiscal tempo knocks you out of rhythm.

Budgets bring harmony and propel you toward additional financial decluttering—assessing your current money situation and addressing any messes (think debt, unpaid bills, piles of receipts, and unclear goals). When you both see in writing what you are spending, one, if not both of you, will have a visceral reaction. Aghast at how much you've both spent at restaurants or on unread magazine subscriptions, you'll inevitably eliminate certain expenses. This reality check may require winnowing away at categories because you've agreed to stop spending more than you make. Fewer expenses are easier to manage and have an important marriage-building impact. Write fewer checks, have more sex. This maxim isn't just true because it rhymes; it's true because check-writing is a stressful distraction that drains you of energy that can be spent . . . well, elsewhere.

Don't know where to begin with the budgeting process? While this chapter focuses on practical organizational strategies, we spent an entire chapter focused on our personal budgeting routine in *Slaying the Debt Dragon*.[5] You'll also find free printable budget forms on the *Your Money, Your Marriage* online guide to begin working through the nuts and bolts of your own finances. Once you've worked through a written budget, several financial decluttering tasks remain. Asking and agreeing on answers to the following questions will help.

Am I being kind? Proverbs 18:21 reminds us, "The tongue has the power of life and death." Kindness and empathy with your spouse generate life. Browbeating and criticism kill your chances at success. Begin your conversations with phrases like: "I love you. Let's make a plan together." Listen to your spouse's concerns. Don't talk while they are talking. Ask great questions such as: "How can we best save up for that purchase?" or "What changes can we make to help you have more peace?" Avoid harsh responses including, "You're wrong!" and "I know you're not good at this." Think carefully about the words you're using and the impact those words will have on your marriage.

How often should we have budget meetings? When you and your spouse intentionally review giving, spending, and savings goals together (naked or not), you are having a budget meeting. You should have these "money dates" often. In the beginning, your meetings should be monthly if not weekly. We enjoyed monthly money dates for several years, becoming extraordinarily comfortable with talking about money. Now, after lots of practice and daily communication, Cherie and I have relatively long meetings twice a year. We forecast our spending and financial plan six months ahead. Maintaining a long view allows us not to miss semiannual bills like auto and life insurance. However, every single day (sometimes multiple times a day), we discuss the flow of money in and out of our home.

Where do you put your bills? Bypass an ignored kitchen drawer. Designate a place paper bills can call home. Ensure you and your spouse know and understand where unpaid bills belong. Agree to pay the bills on time to avoid late fees like the plague.

How do you enter receipts? I'll confess, every now and again my wallet houses stacks of receipts. Fortunately, Cherie reviews the online bank account at least once a day and knows in real time when I've made a purchase. She then enters these receipts into our financial management software, Quicken. Other useful tools include Microsoft Money, Dave Ramsey's Every Dollar, You Need a Budget, Mint.com, and Mvelopes. Enter receipts into your expense-tracking system or paper check register as soon as possible.

Do I need a filing cabinet? Is it 1973? Clutter is clutter even if you can't see it. Out of sight, out of mind is one of the most dangerous mantras in personal finance. Personally, we keep one month's worth of physical billing statements in a Wonder Woman bucket on Cherie's desk. Since all our regular bills, bank accounts, and investments allow access online, there's no need for piles of hard copies. When a new physical bill arrives, the old one gets tossed. You should, however, keep original car titles, life and auto insurance policies, property deeds, wills, advance directives, birth certificates, and at least one statement from each of your financial entities in a safe spot, like a fireproof box. Don't forget to organize your digital finances too. We keep the sites of our bills and investments bookmarked on the home computer's web browser.

How often do you "balance the checkbook"? Stay on top of it. Unless you don't make transactions, daily is the safest solution. A few minutes a day will save you hours later. Our parents' generation typically did this automatically when writing a new check, keeping a paper register of income and expenses. Even if your bank automatically reconciles your accounts in an app or financial software, you need to confirm what you've spent and earned. Both spouses need to make a regular practice of logging in and seeing account balances to prevent overdrawing, overspending, and miscommunication.

Should we automate? Paying bills takes time. Automation does the work for you and avoids late fees. If you place utility bills on automatic withdrawal, confirm you will always have enough money to pay them. If your income varies, realize these basic needs come first before other spending. Regular budgeting ensures there will be enough money in the account to keep the lights on and water flowing. For utility bills that seasonally fluctuate, research options like budget billing. A utility company estimates your bill in advance and averages the amount over twelve months. A consistent, fixed amount simplifies your family budget.

Should we use envelopes? Made popular by Dave Ramsey but in existence decades before, the envelope system is a method of organizing and protecting your day-to-day budget.[6] The basic concept involves placing a set amount of cash in separate paper envelopes earmarked for different areas of spending: groceries, dining out, entertainment, clothing, etc. As we shared in chapter three, you spend less with cash than with debit or especially credit cards.[7] Consumers often assume credit cards promote responsible spending and offer worthwhile rewards like airline miles, cash back, or online discounts. But data shows that credit card users actually spend more money than if they used cash, which negates the value of the rewards from these programs.[8]

The envelope system blocks you from overspending through what psychologists call the partition effect. When anything is wrapped up into smaller parts, consumption decreases. Whether cookies, chips, or cash, dividing the entire lot into individual portions causes a person to stop and think before binging.[9] So using envelopes to protect your spending is a smart strategy to stay on budget.

Even if you opt for digital "envelopes," you train your brain to keep from going overboard. For savings purposes, we have separate online banking accounts for categories like Christmas spending, vacation, vehicle maintenance and repair, and household updates. Placing a set percentage of our income into these "envelopes" rather than leaving the money in our checking account helps us to routinely save money toward financial goals.[10]

What's the Matter with the Mess? Or the Berenstain Bears and Too Much Stuff: Cherie

Picture it. 1984. Rural Indiana. First-grade Cherie sits at a one-piece molded desk in a dusty classroom of a three-story red brick schoolhouse built in 1910. Longingly, she glances around at the other desks, many donned with the coveted "Neat as a Pin" award. While she received many decorations that year, including the revered "Quiet as a Mouse" honor, this elusive accolade always seemed to escape her grasp. It wasn't that she wanted to be messy; it was just that her brain always exploded with a new, exciting adventure, leaving little time to clean up the aftereffects from the last one. A desk stuffed sidewise with pencils, papers, crayons, books, and all varieties of glue (stick, bottled, and paste) quelled each attempt at tidiness.

Neatness (or lack thereof) remains a lifelong struggle for me. Messy lockers followed messy desks, and messy dorm rooms trotted along after that. Then came marriage and babies and the mess grew and grew. Toys mated and multiplied like rabbits. Dishes piled high in the sink. Mount Saint Laundry towered in a tangled mess. Many times the mess led to losing some crucial items; I'm confident we spent three of the first fifteen years of our marriage looking for my keys.

But no matter how much I struggle with the task of keeping things straight, one truth remains: physical mess is distracting. Clutter keeps us from finding what we need, causes us to waste time, and prevents us from focusing on what truly matters. Environments set the mood for financial foreplay. No couple accomplishes financial goals while buried in chaos and jumbled record keeping. "Experts say that in the U.S., 15 to 20% of our annual income is drained by disorganized finances."[11] So if your household income comes in at $50,000 per year, you could be wasting $7,500 to $10,000 due to clutter each year. Nearly a quarter of all Americans pay their bills late because they can't find them. Over 10 percent of households rent storage units to contain extra stuff that won't fit in their homes. As a nation, we spend close to an hour a day looking for things we own but can't find. In the end, we purchase duplicate items. Last but not least, food waste can total up to $2,275 per year for a family of four.[12]

Likewise, the mess diminishes your sex life. Imagine planning the quintessential romantic evening with your spouse. What would your space look like? Maybe you imagine a beautiful bed covered in red rose petals, soft mood lighting, and the lilting notes of lovely music filling the air. My best guess is that your ideal evening doesn't include staring at stacks of things you don't even want and a pile of old clothes you meant to donate six months ago. If you're like most Americans, you own too much stuff, and stuff disorients marriages while simultaneously emptying checkbooks.

During the last decade, home organization has morphed into an idol for our culture. As the previous god of collecting more and more stuff was found left wanting, we developed a thirst for keeping all of the stuff in check. The demand for storage units, stores specializing in containers, and expert organizers skyrocketed. Authors penned bestsellers and producers developed hit TV series all based on managing our personal property and what happens when owning too much spirals out of control.

What is it about marriage that attracts complete and total opposites? The introvert falls head over heels for the extrovert. The spontaneous spirit captivates the calculating character. The pragmatist and the dreamer, the artist and the scientist, the woo girl and the altar boy, the bad boy and the girl next door—the list of contradicting couples stretches more than a mile long. Plausibly, in your marriage one of you tends to keep things nice and neat while the other is more comfortable with the mess. Right now all of the Neat Nicks are doing a happy dance, hoping that I'm going to *finally* convince Messy Mary to clean it up. Or maybe it's Messy Marvin who needs to do a clean sweep before he can sweep Neat Norah off her feet.

In the same ways Brian talked about decluttering your money, learning to manage the mess in your home depends on moving toward better practices, not converting your spouse to your specific system or view of the world. You must budge toward each other, physically and metaphorically in the midst of the mess. For most of us this process is, well, messy. Merging your collective upbringing and personal habits into one requires give and take. Often you might not have known there was even a problem until you got into a spat over the matter. Been there, done that.

The clutter in your home causes chaos in your finances and misery in the marital bed. In my pursuit to curb my own poor choices and habits, I did a little research on untidiness. I considered consulting *New York Times* bestselling author Marie Kondo to investigate the KonMari method. But in the end, I settled on a trusted duo of authorities from my childhood—Jan and Stan Berenstain. In their seminal work, *The Berenstain Bears Think of Those in Need*, Jan and Stan outline the agonizing struggle so many families face—the battle of too much stuff. The ever-savvy Mama Bear plots to rid her home of all the extra toys, games, fishing poles, and even a few items of her own. The family chooses to give the items they no longer use to other bears in need (we'll save the discussion of how maybe they should have given new items to those down on their luck for another day). The book closes with the Bear family riding home in that glorious convertible red roadster, feeling all warm and fuzzy for their generosity but giving holiday store displays the side-eye, lusting after the new items they now want to buy.[13]

You and I aren't too much different from those grizzlies. We endeavor to dump the junk, but as soon as it's gone, we find ourselves in want of new stuff to take its place. And so the binging and purging cycle repeats itself over and over again as we haul out plastic garbage bags filled with used items and then bring in more plastic bags from department stores and big-box retailers. In the end, the stuff is never enough, and the outward messiness reflects the inward state of our souls.

Your external situation mirrors your internal condition. This is why the mess matters. For those of us who struggle with order, it's easy to be dismissive of disorder. After all, what's on the inside always counts more than what's on the outside, right? Yes and no. Our physical surroundings both flow from and then influence financial foreplay. The cyclical outgrowth of chaos repeats the course of action ad nauseam until intimacy is impossible. Clutter clogs the space between husbands and wives. There's no room for a shared vision or a shared bed in the middle of physical and financial turmoil.

And so for the Messy Marys like me, admitting that the mess matters is the first step in a healing journey of moving from being scattered to becoming more organized. Note: I said *becoming* organized. We're all works in progress. Taking that first step of acceptance isn't enough. We have to begin to dig through the mess, allowing God to refine our hearts and homes in the process. Yes, the discombobulated state of our homes and checkbooks emulate the condition of our marriages and money. But the good news remains: we don't have to live like that anymore.

What I Learned from Holiday Barbie: Brian

Before becoming parents, without disagreement, we decided against one classic toy. We pledged our daughters would never possess a Barbie doll. Unfortunately, our rationale doesn't merit a footnote in this tale. Alas, this story is about how indeed our daughters never owned a Barbie, all while someone else in our house violated the prohibition. Nothing frustrates kids more than parental hypocrisy. I'm guessing there's a special level of exasperation for a little girl who can't have Barbie and finds out that Dad had one all along. That's right, I broke the rule. It was me. I know, you're thinking, "Dude?" Allow me to explain (cause it sure isn't justified).

Early in my college career I worked at a major toy retailer. Surrounded by toys and collectibles, the store had its regulars who would sift through Hot Wheels, baseball cards, and figurine shipments upon arrival, searching for a rare commodity. But the most heralded event of the year centered around the release of the holiday Barbie. Long-time employees shared war stories about the long lines and intense customers desperate for her majestic annual reveal. People be crazy. And, as it turns out, I am people.

One year during production of the doll, the factory burned to the ground, severely limiting production. As a capitalist, it didn't take me long to decipher basic principles of supply and demand. If collectors fought over a normal supply of holiday Barbies every year, surely they would clamber at the opportunity to obtain one when the supply was sliced in half. With direct access to the distribution channel and some backroom dealing, I procured one of these white whales in all her holiday glory. Straight from the supplier, Barbie remained in mint condition, protected by the brown cardboard shipping box. I stood prepared to profit a fortune.

Apparently, I'm not a great capitalist. While I possessed a high-demand, low-supply good, I had no way to find the market. Resale sites like eBay, Craigslist, and social media didn't exist. So Barbie stayed in her box, got packed up when we got married, moved with us three times, and occupied a darkened closet shelf. Pride hindered me from just cutting my losses. Twenty or so years later, a friend sold Barbie for me on eBay to a guy in Australia. I made almost six dollars—a terrible return on investment.

We've all undervalued or overvalued something. For me, a grown man, it was an overvalued frilly doll designed for children. Sunk cost and what experts call the endowment effect erroneously convinced me the Barbie was worth more than it was, simply because I owned it. We develop strange and unexplainable attachments to inanimate objects for a number of reasons. To move toward a more organized life, we must correctly value spending, stuff, time, space, and people.

Nothing testifies to what you truly value more than your spending habits. *Out of the heart, the wallet speaks.* Critically examining three months' worth of spending evidences your values. Maybe you love Thai food more than charitable giving or the nail salon more than dinner out with your spouse. Does your spending align with the shared values you and your spouse decided on in chapter five? Dollars reveal our hearts.

As part of my job as a family law attorney, I see men and women going through a divorce face the daunting task of assigning a value to their personal property. I've seen folks fight over toasters and towels. Once in fifteen years, a couple initially valued their household furnishings correctly. Once. We overvalue our stuff because we focus on what we paid and potential replacement cost as opposed to garage-sale value. The unpleasant reality is your stuff's all going to the landfill someday, so your home is filled with future trash. Ouch. When we view possessions through a value-based lens, we begin to accumulate less. By amassing less stuff, we free resources for our shared dreams.

Time is how we make money. Whether it's your hourly rate or interest on an investment account, money multiplies with time. If you don't understand the value of money, you won't understand the value of anything else—including your spouse. How long do you and/or your spouse have to work to buy something?

According to the US Census Bureau, the median household income in 2015 was $56,516.[14] My rough math indicates the number equates to about twenty-seven dollars per hour. For any purchase or expense, the median-incomed family would divide the cost by twenty-seven dollars to determine how many hours one or both would have to work for that purchase. Instead of working for things, work for each other.

The more expenses you have, the less value you place on your time. In essence, you're communicating concepts like I'd rather have a new car with a five-hundred-dollar-per-month payment than see my spouse more. Time is money. When we choose more expensive goods, we choose to work more hours in our lifetime. Five hundred dollars per month could prevent anniversary vacations or earlier retirement, potentially years of time spent together as a couple. That money properly invested leads to more shared time. Reducing spending and eliminating stuff buys you time. Value your time and protect it. Because time is so valuable, don't waste it or fritter it away. Be intentional with your time as it relates to your shared needs, values, and dreams.

Space also has a value. Billions of dollars are spent every year on storage facilities because people have filled their space with stuff they don't need. If your home has a value, the space inside your home has a value as well. Hopefully you wouldn't pay someone else to store the clothes you haven't worn in six years. But you, in effect, are paying for it. Look around your home and ask yourself if your present possessions are the best use of your space. Open space in your home means you manage less and decrease the likelihood of cash-sucking clutter.

Above all else, value people. Your spouse holds more value than stuff, time, and space combined. The Bible instructs us how we should measure the value of our lives: "However, I consider my life worth nothing to me; my only aim is to finish the race and complete the task the Lord Jesus has given me—the task of testifying to the good news of God's grace" (Acts 20:24).

We often think of sharing the good news of God's grace to unidentifiable masses, forgetting to testify to the one right in front of us. Your spending, your stuff, your time, and your space should all reflect God's grace to your husband or wife. If everything in your home is cluttered and broken, your home may be mirroring your marriage and your souls. Lift one another up by focusing on true value and not being distracted by worthless pursuits.

Let's Get Practical: Cherie

I'm a morning person. While I enjoy sleeping in as much as the next girl, getting out of bed isn't really a struggle for me. Embracing the joy and blank slate of a new day, I love making breakfast and beginning again. Everything seems ripe with potential. But odds are good I'd be much less Pollyanna if I didn't have my favorite Wonder Woman mug filled with the warm and delicious nectar sponsoring my early a.m. optimism—coffee.

My coffee obsession began in college when I discovered just how amazing this miracle beverage tasted and made me feel. Local coffee houses fueled long nights of study before Starbucks claimed every campus for its own. I favored a specific espresso drink named Rocket Fuel, which might explain my flirtations with high blood pressure now, but I digress. Mornings and coffee go together like peas and carrots, like Forrest and Jen-nae.

For this reason, before I go to bed at night, I ritualistically prepare our cherry red Hamilton Beach. Grounds and filter fixed, water filled, and timer programmed fifteen minutes before my alarm clock will ring, the mechanism for delivering my daily cup of happy juice depends on preparation. Doing things in advance—for your money and your marriage—is a lot like setting a coffee pot the night before. You commit to forethought and some basic legwork. But the outcome brews with beauty, delivering the energy and vitality you need to make it through another day.

Organization requires advance action. Odds are good you didn't create your physical and financial clutter overnight, so you won't be able to twitch your nose or wave a magic wand to remove the mess instantaneously either. The endeavor necessitates daily planned motion conducted over time. Just like nightly setting the coffee pot, you'll have to do things on a routine basis. You'll need to anticipate busy seasons and potential pitfalls. And you'll need to take action so you won't be found without a drop in your mug each morning.

One of my absolute favorite verses in the Bible is Proverbs 22:3. *The Message* beautifully updates its ancient wisdom in modern terms. "A prudent person sees trouble coming and ducks; a simpleton walks in blindly and is clobbered." To avoid more of a mess in the future and remain organized, you must see trouble coming. If you don't keep an eye out for crisis, you'll be walloped upside the head.

Talk is cheap in this organizational madness though. Here are some concrete strategies to help you control the clutter in your home so nothing comes between you and your spouse except the bed sheets.

Purge with three boxes. In your problem areas, line up three boxes. Designate one as a Give Box and place items inside that you plan on donating to a charity or people you know who could use the extras. The second box is your Keep Box. Inside of it, deposit anything you know you want to keep but need to find a permanent home for. Finally, toss everything else in the Trash Box (or maybe bag).

Everything has its home. During his childhood, Brian's dad taught him several valuable lessons. Your keys go in your left front pocket. Your change lives in your right front pocket. Your wallet needs to be placed in your right rear pocket, and your comb gets put in the left rear pocket. And if you put all those items where they belong in random succession, you come close to doing half the Macarena. The underlying organizational strategy becomes priceless when applied throughout your home. Valuables need homes. If you're constantly losing your keys, you need one set space you return them to each time you come home. This simple strategy added minutes to my day and hours to my life.

Can it be replaced in twenty minutes and for less than twenty dollars? I love tips on minimalism. One of the key concepts I picked up from The Minimalists, Joshua Fields Millburn and Ryan Nicodemus, early on is what they call the 20/20 Principle.[15] If we're on the fence about keeping or pitching something, we ask ourselves if the item could be replaced in twenty minutes and for less than twenty dollars. If the answer is yes, we go ahead and pass the item along. A simple litmus test like this can help you cut down on the extras cluttering your cabinets and clogging your closets.

Talk to each other about money daily. Brian's already shared specific strategies for budgeting earlier in this chapter, but be sure that part of your daily rhythm includes conversations about money. Think through future expenses, discuss charges or deposits cleared, and see "trouble coming" in the form of field trips, birthdays, holidays, sports fees, and more.

Set a dollar limit for nonbudgeted purchases. To avoid financial clutter, you need to communicate and then overcommunicate about what you're buying. This simple practice prevents overdrawing and overbuying. While we were paying off $127,000 in debt, Brian and I decided that for any nonbudgeted purchase over ten dollars, we would talk to each other first. I know this might seem drastic, but it's what worked for us. What's important is that you both choose a dollar amount you agree on. It's rare that one of us (in fact I can't think of a single occasion) has said no when we've touched base on an unexpected purchase. It's not about controlling each other's spending but about keeping in constant financial contact.

Communicate three times more than usual when it comes to major purchases. Again, to steer clear of financial chaos, be sure you and your spouse go above and beyond when it comes to talking about making a major purchase. Note: communication is not ranting, nagging, selling, convincing, or trying to get your way. Winning is understanding the other's concerns and needs and coming to a common conclusion.

Buy less, have more sex. This is our favorite perk of minimalism. If you don't have too much stuff (to store, clean, move, repair, etc.), you won't be overwhelmed by the organizational process. When you own less, you free up physical space in your home and aren't constantly battling clutter. You'll spend less time looking for things and less time cleaning. You may even argue less. Unencumbered, you should be able to focus on what really matters—people, not things. Make your purchases based on what you need and not what you want. You may just find more space to breathe and more time for sex.

Come Together

The most sacred space of your marriage could be the messy middle ground. Husbands and wives are unlikely to ever become carbon copies of one another, agreeing on every home organization strategy. One spouse probably will never win the "Neat as a Pin" award, while the other will rack up honor after honor. But the movement of working together to manage your living space and your finances enhances intimacy.

Collaboration knits your souls together as you tackle the problem as one. As we budge toward one another, the barriers of our physical and financial messes begin to melt away. We're drawn into a sweeter intimacy when chaos dissipates. Managing and maintaining a home together challenges even the most stable couples. But understanding the value of our stuff (or lack thereof) helps us better place a priority on the person we've pledged to spend life with until death do us part. After all, your husband or wife is worth more than chaos and mess and yet worth more than perfect order too.

A new day dawns when we all agree we could do a better job at clearing out physical and financial clutter. When couples work together to bring order to their homes and their bank accounts, it clears and frees their energy for heightened intimacy.

Discussion Questions

1. Describe the first home you shared as a married couple. What were the biggest lessons you learned in the first nine months of your marriage?
2. Why might it be important to declutter your money *before* you declutter your home?
3. How can your physical mess keep you from managing your money well? How can your financial mess contribute to physical mess? How does either (or both) affect romance in your marriage?

4. "If you don't understand the value of money, you won't understand the value of anything else—including your spouse." How does understanding the true value of money and our possessions cause us to place a higher priority on our husbands and wives?
5. Which practical organization strategy for money or stuff resounded with you most? What others would you add?

Fostering Financial Foreplay

- Use the budget forms from the *Your Money, Your Marriage* online guide to begin the work of decluttering your money—together. Make out for five minutes after completing each worksheet.
- Find three boxes and choose one area of your home—a closet, a cabinet, a desk, or a set of drawers—to begin the process of purging. P.S. You're only allowed to put your own stuff in the Trash Box, not your spouse's. After you've finished the job, celebrate by taking a walk together, sharing a bowl of ice cream, or slow dancing in your newly organized space.

CHAPTER 8

What Are You Missing?

From the Fear of Missing Out to the Love of Showing Up

Comparison is the thief of joy.

THEODORE ROOSEVELT

In April 2013, *FOMO* (or the fear of missing out) landed with a thud on a page in the *Oxford English Dictionary.* A recent, expanded definition describes the term as "the uneasy and sometimes all-consuming feeling that you're missing out—that your peers are doing, in the know about, or in possession of more or something better than you."[1]

The experience itself seems ancient. Surely the first cave couple upon returning to their prehistoric class reunion noted their former friends had larger clubs and a mastery of fire, while they still grappled with the best method to chip away on their feeble attempts at making a wheel. Or the early Romans envied townhomes boasting spacious baths belonging to their neighbors down the street, fearing missing out on a more luxurious experience. A bigger ox, a larger cabin, more money, wider influence, greater power—the desire to have what someone else owns or to experience what they're experiencing pulsed in our veins before a single social media feed ever opened.

FOMO finds power in jealousy—a struggle that led Cain to kill his brother Abel. And those desires of "I would be so much better off if I had ___________" trace all the way back to the first couple, Adam and Eve. While modern technology may have amplified the anxiety or provided more opportunities for exposure, the struggle existed in the beginning.

Our parents still felt the pangs of missing out when they received a Christmas letter or gathered with long-lost friends or gazed at an eighties sitcom where the squeaky-clean family depicted never seemed to really work but still lived in a marvelous home. Our grandparents and great-grandparents, many who lived through the lean years of the Great Depression, weren't granted contentment simply because they grew up with little. The human soul always seems to find itself in a place of want, in a longing for more, in fear of missing out.

But from now on, for generations to come, we are faced with livestreamed knowledge of everything we lack—from the vacation we can't afford, to the fancy meal we won't be eating, to the party we weren't invited to. Painfully, we scroll ad nauseam and probably even stop to take a moment to "like" a post, even though, if we were completely honest, our feelings were much less than positive. We're still waiting for Facebook to release the "I wish I had what you have" emoticon. Our best guess is that won't happen anytime soon.

What happens when the fear of missing out intersects with our marriages? I'm sure you've seen the scenario play out in the relationships of friends and family members. At best, couples end up drowning in debt, trying to pay for possessions and experiences they can't afford. At worst, they end up sleeping with someone else, attempting to satisfy the "grass is always greener" syndrome.

How can anyone battle FOMO? Will merely killing the newsfeed end the madness? Or is the ancient struggle embedded in our souls, with no hope of relief? Cultivating a marriage and money outlook that moves from the fear of missing out to the love of showing up requires quitting.

When you quit longing for someone else's life, you find contentment in your own. When you quit longing for someone else's marriage, you realize what you have is so much better—the marriage God crafted specifically for you.

The Secret of the One-Day Diet: Brian

The following story contains two major marketing products: (1) the George Foreman Grill and (2) the Atkins Diet.

When our first New Year's Eve as a married couple rolled around, Cherie and I, the genius but young newlyweds, made a New Year's resolution. It was also our last New Year's resolution. Just a few short weeks before January 1, we browsed a discount bookstore. For reasons that escape me to this day, I purchased a book about eliminating all sugar from your diet. The nation was on the cusp of the low-carb/no-carb craze that would soon vex pizza buffets everywhere. The book explained how carbohydrates turned into sugar and how sugar negatively affected the body. Central to the theme was removing all carbohydrates, sans the occasional berry.

Confusing my political science degree with a degree in actual science, it sounded like a no-brainer. I proposed to Cherie that we give it a shot. I'm sure the aftermath made her regret accepting any other proposal I had made.

Before we embarked on this journey of inevitable health, happiness, and prosperity, we decided to be all in. In the apartment below ours lived two young women, whom we referred to as the "kids" downstairs. Mind you, we were twenty-three. Early that morning, we loaded a box with every starch in our sketchy little apartment and walked it down a flight of stairs to the "kids." The "kids" stood speechless and confused as we delivered pounds of flour, sugar, cereal, bread, and a store of other staples. We explained as best we could that not only were we healthy but we were generous and humble.

Going without sugar or carbohydrates wasn't terrible for the first eleven minutes or so. Plus, we had received a new George Foreman Grill for Christmas that would solve all our problems. But by the end of the day, we were sick to the point that I can't even describe it in this book. It was awful. We contemplated going to the emergency room to avoid dehydration. Now, you may be thinking, *I've never heard of one day going without carbohydrates making someone sick, let alone violently ill.* We're not sure what happened. Was 95 percent of our prior diet composed of refined sugar? Yes. Did we not know how to cook chicken on the George Foreman Grill? Probably. Did I eat a tub of low-carb whipped topping on a blueberry in one sitting? Yes. Yes, I did.

Ultimately, we purged ourselves of sugar because we were afraid of missing out on a hot new diet and the hot new bodies it would surely provide. After all, the book said all our "peers"—the healthy people who conquered carbs and shed pounds—led storybook, successful lives. Concerned my life would be miserable if I missed out, I altered everything about the way I ate.

Our FOMO led to serious pain. FOMO's agony resonated for years to come. FOMO often leads to overcorrection. You see something someone else has or are convinced there is something you should be doing, and you go overboard. When you overcorrect, you're sending a signed invitation for drama, failure, and misery to visit your life.

In our scenario please be reminded that the next day we had no food. We had given it away. We burned the ships so we couldn't turn back. Our sickened selves subsequently bought new ships—more specifically, all the sweetsies we could find. I can safely say that those extra groceries were not in the budget, because we didn't have a budget. Our credit card balance increased and compounded our already destitute existence.

The aftershock of the no-carb day still resonates in our lives. Any time we start something new or try to make a big change, we both think, *Are we just going sugar-free again?* I'm convinced that one day prevented us from starting our debt-free journey as soon as we should have. It may still be preventing us from subtracting or adding something to our lives. Had we heeded the truth of 1 Timothy 4:7, we might have avoided the whole perilous plight and its enduring emanations. "Have nothing to do with godless myths and old wives' tales; rather, train yourself to be godly."

FOMO hampers your decision-making and convinces you to dive headfirst into ill-advised ventures. This increases your risk of failure, financial ruin, and/or hospitalization. Experience is a brutal but honest teacher. Fad diets and "get rich quick" schemes are silly, godless myths which promise fast results to problems that require long-term solutions. These myths stem from FOMO preying on our fear, laziness, and impatience. For us, fear rather than fitness fueled our efforts, and we failed. We certainly learned several tough lessons, but fortunately it was early in our marriage. In fact, we're still learning to this day. To combat FOMO, one of the questions we use to filter marriage, money, and parenting decisions is, "What's the endgame?" This question helps reorient our priorities and distinguish between a decision that has positive long-term consequences and another "no-carb day." *If you want your future to be better than your past, change your present.* However, overcorrection will wreck your future instead of changing it for the better. Make incremental changes over time, born of love, not fear. Also, consider purchasing a meat thermometer.

Identity Theft: Cherie

Mirror, mirror, on the wall . . . who's the fairest of them all?

They're classic words from a child's fairy tale that should strike more fear in our hearts than they do. Perhaps because they come from make-believe characters or maybe because they have a catchy rhyming rhythm, we gloss over just how startling the words of Snow White's wicked stepmother queen are.

She is desperate for someone else's life. After all, this woman will go so far as to hire a hitman and eventually poison her own stepchild, all so she can steal an identity: the fairest in the land. The wicked queen had one of the maddest cases of FOMO I've ever seen. Her all-consuming fear of one in possession of greater beauty drove her homicidal. It's pretty messed up and slightly terrifying that we read such stories to our own children just before they drift off at night, right?

Sleep well, kid. Sleep well.

I'm guessing if we were allowed an audience with the queen, she'd have all the "right" reasons for her choices and deny she was after someone else's world, or feared missing out. After all, she wanted what was rightfully hers to begin with, you know? The fear of missing out sneaks up on us like that. We don't even realize what we're doing until it's gone way too far. And maybe we've done the unthinkable in the name of acquiring what's not ours too.

We've purchased the home decor we knew we couldn't afford to create a space straight from HGTV.

We've gone upside down on a new set of wheels straight from the pages of a magazine.

We've bought the overpriced designer dress for our daughter at the online or home party in a moment of weakness—the one she's certain to outgrow in a matter of months.

The internet ad beckons to us: you need me, you want me, you must buy me. So we click and we order.

Perhaps most disturbing of all, some imagine a "better" life in someone else's marriage. He's so sensitive and caring. She's so smoking hot and never complains. And so we dip our toes into the waters of temptation, and we flirt. Or maybe we're not even that bold. Maybe we just drift off into a daydream about another world, another life, where there are never dirty dishes in the sink or dirty laundry (physical and metaphorical) hidden behind closed doors, where that other person meets each and every one of our needs while also sporting a six-pack.

Regarding her work *Rising Strong*, author Brené Brown breaks down the struggle with our quiet identity-theft longings and predicts its ultimate result: "The 'fear of missing out' is what happens when scarcity slams into shame. FOMO lures us out of our integrity with whispers about what we could or should be doing. FOMO's favorite weapon is comparison. It kills gratitude and replaces it with 'not enough.'"[2]

Fearing that you'll miss out results in never having enough. You'll never be enough. You'll never own enough. You'll never be loved enough. It's a bleak conclusion to our life's pursuits, one that in some cases leads to bankruptcy, affairs, and divorce. And just like the wicked queen, we've gone too far before we even realize we're there.

FOMO finds its roots in jealousy and envy—ancient struggles of the human soul. Still, it's unwise to skip over the ways modern modes of the fear of missing out sneak into our everyday interactions on social media. Our apps and online platforms can be a hot, stinking cesspool of temptation, where we begin dreaming of having what everyone else has. We need to fight the temptation to overcorrect though. The internet itself isn't to blame.

Social media (not unlike money) is a tool. You can use a hammer to build a house or you can choose to throw a hammer through a plate-glass window and cause great destruction. The choice is up to you. Knowing how to properly use a tool, like a hammer or money, requires both head knowledge and practice. Keep at the forefront of your mind the original design of the tool and its best use. Never mindlessly wield a tool like a hammer or money—or for the purposes of our discussion, social media. Using a tool without thought results in destruction and injury. Look away while swinging a hammer and the only thing you're going to nail is your thumb. Click away on the internet without thought, and the only thing you might nail is someone else's spouse.

Can we get down to brass tacks and discuss two platforms where I struggle? The first, because I am a woman in her forties (the median age of its users), is Pinterest. It boasts 150 million active monthly users, who store away ideas for recipes, personal finance,

DIY hacks, exercises, and more. So I'm guessing you might engage in a little pinning fun too. I'll say it outright from the beginning—I love Pinterest. I typically head to Pinterest to search for how to do something before I use a search engine. The practicality and visual nature of this platform appeal to me.

If I'm honest, I know I've fallen into the trap of Pinterest becoming my version of reading trashy romance novels. To be clear, I'm not pinning images of hunky, chiseled men standing on the edge of a cliff. There's another fiction at hand.

Pinterest, just like trashy romance novels or even romantic comedies, can warp our sense of reality. Unaware, we begin to set unrealistic expectations of epic proportions for our husbands, kids, homes, and even our own bodies after only a few minutes of scrolling through the beautifully arranged images. We think that everyone lives inside a picture-perfect world, one where there's always sunshine, no one ever gets sick, homes remain spotless, and each person can hold a plank for fifteen whole minutes.

It's not real. If we're not careful, Pinterest arouses longings that are destructive forces in our lives. We know Pinterest itself isn't evil. It can be used for good, say if you're looking for a way to save money at the grocery store or feed your family on fewer dollars, or even to get ideas for DIY home decor. What's in your heart makes the difference. Are you scrolling because of FOMO, because of envy? Or are you simply looking for a picture-framing tutorial and able to sign off later without having your self-worth reoriented? In the end, the ways we engage with social media say more about the conditions of our hearts than the platforms themselves.

Social media area number two where I seem to dive off the FOMO deep end, I tend to unfairly blame on Mark Zuckerberg. After all, while he may have invented Facebook, he doesn't force my hands to scroll through status after status each day. It's easy for me to fall into a never-ending rabbit hole of vacation photos, articles, memes, and videos on a regular basis. Minutes and hours drift by while I keep up with old and new friends but still sometimes find myself wishing for someone else's life.

As data on social media habits develops, it's no surprise research has uncovered a crucial connection between Facebook usage and mental health. For some, heavy Facebook use results in jealousy and even depression.[3] It's on us to monitor our own behavior and put intentional stops in our own way so we don't fall into an inescapable trap. We can't blame social media for our FOMO hang-ups. We'd have them even without our smartphones. Ditching technology might help you clear up some of the problem, but until we realize our identity issues run much deeper, we won't come out on the other side of the magic mirror liking what we see.

The evil queen longed for Snow White's beauty. She feared missing out on being the fairest in the land, a badge she wore with honor. In my own life, if not careful, I find myself scrolling with a mindset of scarcity. Afraid I'll be left sad and lonely in my marriage or family, I listen to the ugly lies shame whispers. I begin to think buying a cuter dress or new furniture can fill the holes in my soul only Jesus can fill. The sooner I realize FOMO is gripping my heart, the quicker I can defuse it by naming it for what it is. Then I can consciously switch gears to begin drawing contentment from what I have and who I've been made to be.

Train Yo' Self: Brian

I sold us the first car we bought after we were debt-free. Yes, you read that right. I'm not sure if this makes me a great salesman or someone who will buy something from anyone. Our home rests on a main thoroughfare, and friends periodically call on us to sell their car in our driveway. Aside from being a professional wrestling ring announcer, there is no other job I'd enjoy more than selling devalued, previously loved cars. Over the years, no car has gone unsold. So when my friend Brent asked for some valuable driveway space, I was happy to help.

One Sunday afternoon, a fella on a fancy motorcycle pulled into my drive to take a look at Brent's simple gray sedan. While not obligated to greet customers at my makeshift car lot, it's automatic for me. Motorcycle Fella was looking at the car for his teenage daughter. The one-sided conversation proceeded as follows, "Motorcycle Fella, the car has some quirks, but it's my friend Brent's car. He's on the city council, I was the best man in his wedding, and he used to work as a mechanic. There are few people I trust more. It was Grandpa Harry's car before he passed away. Grandpa Harry barely drove, that's why the miles are so low. He was part of the greatest generation, served in WWII, and detailed every mile between every oil change on a log in the console. It's a once-in-a-lifetime grandpa car, the white whale of used car buyers. My wife says that my truck is unsafe at any speed, so I should probably buy this car. There's no reason not to buy it . . . yeah, I'm going to buy it. It was nice meeting you, Motorcycle Fella, but the car is sold."

Everything I told Motorcycle Fella was true. He rode away bewildered by our exchange, and I ended up the proud owner of a 2000 Chevrolet Malibu, along with Grandpa Harry's extensive log. The Malibu did indeed have some quirks, all of which Brent had disclosed to me. It served its purpose well while on the road. One of its limitations, however, was literally getting it on the road. It turned out that the Malibu came equipped with a factory defect in the anti-theft system. At the unpredictable, randomized frequency of a temperamental toddler, the Malibu would not start. All sensible and traditional diagnoses and perceived remedies could not mend this ailment. In short, the Malibu thought (to the extent that a car could think) I was trying to steal it and would consequently shut down. The red anti-theft light illuminated the dashboard and the Malibu precluded the driver from attempting to start it again for ten minutes. For the sake of clarity, this wasn't "around" ten minutes or "a little while"; the Malibu's computer delayed starting for exactly ten minutes to the second.

You may be thinking, that's not a quirk, that's an abomination. Perhaps. But part of me used it as a lesson in planning ahead, since it forced me to leave ten minutes earlier than needed. Part of me, in a twisted, "roulette-wheel gambler" sort of way, enjoyed the heart-racing thrill of not knowing if my car would start. And part of me lost my ever-loving mind due to the Malibu's unreliability. Two unexpected side benefits were the savings on fuel and a more consistent prayer life. I saved money on fuel because I sure wasn't going to tempt fate or increase my odds of anti-theft malfunction by running unnecessary errands. My prayer life improved because I pleaded for God to intercede in the heart of the Malibu at least twice a day: once on the way to work and once on the way home. It was like the stress that comes along with playing the popular board game Pie Face—you know you're going to get hit, you just don't know when. And instead of delicious whipped cream and subsequent laughter, you get hit with being late for work and a bloody tongue from holding back a profanity-laced tirade.

In our culture, waiting ten minutes falls somewhere between a nuisance and aggravation. Increase that to twenty minutes, and aggravation transmutes to misanthropic rage. You see, waiting the prescribed ten minutes did not guarantee the Malibu would start on the second try, or the third. After an adventure at the mall with Zoe and Anna to buy Mother's Day gifts for Cherie, the Malibu failed to start no less than four times. We were leaving the mall because, as the mall can do to you, we were exhausted, spent, and needed to be home. The quirk turned into an enemy and stood in the way of us being where we were supposed to be. Instead of being at home wrapping presents, we were in a mall parking lot, roasting from the unrelenting sun being amplified by the windows of our quirky sedan.

We're all built like the Malibu. Whereas the Malibu shut down when it thought someone was trying to steal it, we shut down and fail to start when we covet something that is not ours. FOMO triggers our internal anti-theft system. FOMO occurs when we're trying to steal someone else's joy, and, as a result, we rob ourselves of the joy God intended for our own lives. When overcome by FOMO, we mire into patterns of trying to live a story not meant for us. As a result, we're locked out of our own calling because we tried to get behind the wheel of someone else's life. Instead of a ten-minute Malibu delay, we could be delayed ten years on our life's intended journey.

Cherie and I have known people who detailed the characteristics of their perfect potential mate (and one fella even named her). The fear of missing out on the fabricated ideal prevented them from dating anyone for most of their adult lives. When I worked retail in college, a frequent customer refused to get a job for the fear of missing out on his potential dream job. Idealizing the perfect spouse, the perfect job, or the perfect house freezes decision-making. A fear of missing out leaves you afraid to make any decisions because you might lose a better opportunity.

Eventually, we resold the Malibu to a man who really needed a car and didn't mind the idea of the anti-theft defect. It wasn't the first time I've sold the same car twice, but that's a separate story. When we sold the Malibu, we solved our anti-theft problems. Conquering FOMO is not as easy. All day notifications, advertisements, and distractions bombard us. Americans between the ages of twenty-five and thirty-four check their phones on average fifty times per day.[4] Teens spend an average of nine hours per day on social media platforms.[5]

We are checking our phones because we're afraid we will miss something. Whatever noble excuse we attach to it, in reality, we just want to see what everyone else is doing. These distractions add up and waste otherwise productive years from your life through the pervasive checking and staring alone. If you do the math based on the facts above, three out of every eight years are spent entirely on social media. Constant stopping and changing course based on the flitters of the day will not just frustrate you and derail your goals; it will make you broke.

When you see your friends on vacation, you want to go on vacation, whether you have the money or not. When you see your grade-school acquaintance post a picture of his new car, you think, *I was always smarter than that guy. He used to eat paste. I should probably have a new car too.* Slowly but surely we can slip into a trap of discontentment, dissatisfied with our possessions. Or an even more dreadful possibility—we become dissatisfied with our spouse.

Selling the Malibu was only part of solving the equation to eliminate the anti-theft issue from my life. The more important factor was buying a new car without the anti-theft defect. It took me a few months to stop panicking prior to starting the engine. Old habits die hard. More often than we realize, quitting does not necessarily abolish the actual problem. Even if it does, we just replace one habit with another. We eradicate fear by exchanging it for something more powerful, more effective, and more reliable.

Moving to the Love of Showing Up

Ridding yourself of FOMO requires what theologian Thomas Chalmers referred to as the "expulsive power of a new affection."[6] Specifically, the new affection Chalmers references is Jesus. Only Jesus expels the habits and sin holding us back from the abundant life we're promised. "There is no fear in love. But perfect love drives out fear" (1 John 4:18). Jesus's love works in our lives at the soul-level where real change occurs.

In our house, we have three basic tenets: Love God. Love people. Show up. It turns out that these three ideologies will also help you avoid FOMO. Let's move from FOMO to the love of showing up (LOSU).

Instead of being afraid of missing out on a hot new restaurant, let's show up at our dinner tables and enjoy the food God has provided for us. Instead of being afraid of missing out on the resort vacation, let's show up in everyday moments with each other. Instead of being afraid of missing out on the newest phone or biggest TV or fanciest home, let's show up and love our actual lives.

It's easy to love people from a distance. Showing up in someone's life at their darkest or most desperate hour is a challenge. I've often missed the boat on this one. Start with the person closest to you, your husband or your wife. Begin serving your spouse in ways that you've long since neglected.

FOMO is not that you consciously think your life will be diminished if you don't know whether the uncle of the guy you once worked on a project with won his fishing tournament or not. The attraction is, in part, biochemical. Every time you log on to social media or respond to a notification, your body gives you a hit of dopamine.[7] Dopamine is a positive reward hormone released from the brain. It's also released with cocaine use. I'm not sure I have to draw the analogy out much further, but compulsively responding to the notifications on your smartphone is addictive.[8]

Replace the negative effects of FOMO by combatting the dopamine rush. Being generous releases the hormone oxytocin, a feel-good chemical of the brain.[9] Instead of checking your smartphone or scrolling through a social media feed, serve your spouse. Give to and serve at your church. Oxytocin also releases during a prolonged hug. We discussed the many benefits of a protracted hug in chapter five. Triumph over FOMO by hugging your spouse instead of checking your smartphone. FYI: oxytocin is released after orgasms too. Sooooo, if your prolonged hug turns horizontal, even better!

If you continue to struggle with FOMO, below is a list of practical tips to help you move from the fear of missing out to the love of showing up:

1. **Know your triggers of desire.** Is it TV, internet, social media, specific people, certain stores, email?
2. **Develop a "Do Not" list.** To-do lists are helpful (and also give you a dopamine hit), but Jim Collins, renowned author of leadership books like *Good to Great* and *Built to Last,* advocates a strategy of making a "Do Not" list. Make a list of things you will not do this week and stick to it.
3. **You may need a social media shutdown.** A complete fast from social media may result in a corresponding binge or it may show you that you can live without it. At a minimum,

go to the settings on your phone and your computer and turn off the notifications so that you are not besieged by technology. You may want to set some notifications for certain people, but you do not need to immediately know when your childhood neighbor goes live from the ice cream shop.

4. **If you spend any time at all on social media, you need to use the hide button more.** Ask yourself if you follow someone on social media to maintain a relationship or if they slipped through your filter.
5. **Spend time with God and your spouse together.** The closer you grow together with your spouse toward God, the less FOMO will be an issue in your money and your marriage.
6. **Make a love list.** Better than a to-do list or a "Do Not" list, the love list is comprised of things you actually love to do. If you are working from that list, you will be less inclined to fall into the FOMO trap.
7. **Your bedroom is sacred; don't bring the smartphone into it.** Get an old-school alarm clock, and charge your phone in the hallway instead. Bringing your smartphone into your bedroom draws attention away from where it needs to be and also inhibits sleep.

But What about My Babies?: Cherie

Within the first few hours of my daughter Anna's life, my mom dropped some serious reality square in my lap. Together as we gazed at the bundle of new life squirming in my arms, she gently said to me, "When you stay home, you will want to work. And when you work, you will want to stay at home." Slightly stunned, perhaps from the lingering pain and subsequent C-section medication, I blinked at her. My new-mom heart deflated a bit, but I've never begrudged my mom for sharing her wisdom in that moment. Over the years as I stayed home full-time, went to grad school full-time, worked part- and full-time, and worked from home, the words rang true.

Perhaps more than any other area, FOMO creeps into the corners of my life most when it comes to parenting. I worry about what I am missing. Could I or should I advance my career? Did my daughter hit a new milestone while in the care of another? How can you truly know if you're doing everything you're supposed to be doing?

And then the fear of missing out dances right over into worries for my kids. Are they in the right schools? Do they have the right friends? Should we be doing dance lessons? Piano lessons? Teaching them Greek, Spanish, and Japanese? What about their artistic pursuits? The right camps? The best birthday parties? Don't even get me started on vacations. Combine these innate worries with the constant presence of social media and real-life acquaintances doing every activity and pursuing every passion under the sun, and I'm left flat-out confused and panicked.

If not careful, all the above can lead to what we like to call the FOMO hop. It's like a 1950s-themed sock hop without the cute poodle skirts and bobby socks. As parents, we're tempted to jump from one thing to the next. This year, little Timmy is going to be a Rhodes Scholar, so we pile on the summer bridge work and beef up his academic curriculum. The next year, we're certain he's the next Ty Cobb, so there's the batting cages and travel teams and private coaching sessions to attend. But wait! We discover he has a knack for the drums, and in an attempt to develop his inner Dave Grohl, we purchase a set of sticks and skins, dishing out more cash for lessons.

FOMO hop is not necessarily confined to the children though. I've fallen victim to it and seen my friends do the same. We start blogs that lay vacant. We train for marathons and then hang up our running shoes after we finish. We sell oils or makeup or leggings or food or bags or jewelry. It's like we're grasping for anything and everything to beat away the terrifying fear that someone else will have what we can't have. We barely set down one pursuit before we pick up the next. We want more, we need more, we can't function without more.

C. S. Lewis, in one of his classic Narnia tales *The Horse and His Boy,* summed up the struggle with these words, "One of the drawbacks about adventures is that when you come to the most beautiful places you are often too anxious and hurried to appreciate them."[10] Don't misunderstand me. There's nothing wrong with vacations or music lessons or running marathons. They can all be great adventures, and if you have the budget to cover the cost, they can lead to wonderful memories. But there's a perilous trap of temptation under our feet if we marry our decisions to fear. In the midst of that anxiety and hurry, we completely miss the most beautiful places of our lives.

When we sacrifice our finances because we're afraid our babies will miss out, everyone suffers. Sure, your child may be able to enjoy Disney World right now, but then you may not be able to handle the cost of college. Or you figure out a way to buy all the presents and lessons and designer clothes but underfund (or don't fund at all) your retirement. More than once, a mom has said to me, "But I don't want my child to pay for my prior financial mistakes. So we're going to go ahead and . . . buy the camper/put the trip on a credit card/you fill in the blank." As you might guess, by compounding one mistake with another, her story never ends well.

Can I be bold? Your child *will* suffer in some form or fashion for your money mistakes. Whether they don't go to Disney World right now because you can't afford it or they end up saddled with caring for you in your old age because you haven't saved for the future, they're likely to feel the impact of your choices. When you let the fear of disappointing someone else (your child, your parents, your friends) or even the fear of disappointing yourself dictate your financial choices, FOMO wins.

I'm not trying to rain on your parade or spoil family fun. But none of us can do everything. The fear of missing out murmurs lies to the contrary. Especially when it comes to parenting, you'll need to make some difficult decisions along the way. You'll be faced with choices and paths. Sometimes you'll have to say no so you can say yes to something else. Moving toward the love of showing up compels us to make the tough call and put on our grown-up pants. We have to realize our limitations in order to raise healthy children.

If you find the parenting/FOMO connection difficult to bear, seek out like-minded parents to aid your journey. Join a small group where you can openly and honestly share your struggles. If your money mentors are parents, tap into that additional wisdom. Seek out a MOPS or moms' community to gain support. And since FOMO has its roots in jealousy and envy, ask a parent, grandparent, or other older adult who influenced your life how they combatted jealousy or learned from their financial mistakes.

Enough Is Enough

Not so long ago we had a conversation with our daughter Anna about the concept of diminishing returns. As all great conversations do, it diverged into a discussion about ice cream. The point was this: If you do exactly what you want to do all the time, you won't be able to do exactly what you want to do.

Think of your favorite ice cream. You can eat ice cream every day for a while. But eventually, your doctor is going to cut you off and medicate you for diabetes. You'll be banished from Baskin-Robbins for the remainder of your life, all because you didn't exercise self-control. The same principle applies to sleep and shopping. You can get away with pulling a few all-nighters, but go a couple of weeks without proper sleep and you've bought yourself a one-way ticket to crazy town. And shopping can be a fun contact sport, but shopping for recreation will eventually deplete your bank account and put you in a situation where you cannot shop at all.

FOMO entices you to do stuff you can't afford. You may get away with it for a little while, but the accumulation of several ordinary expenses over time will push you past the brink. The fear of missing out clouds our judgment, causing short-term emotions to dictate long-term decisions. It's a dangerous trap, a slippery slope, and a ticking time bomb waiting to blow up your marriage.

When you learn to move toward the love of showing up—toward enjoying what you have instead of longing for what you don't—you realize you don't want or need anyone else's life, stuff, or spouse. You already have the abundant life you were created to live. You already have the husband or wife God gave specifically to you. You already have enough.

Discussion Questions

1. Brian and Cherie filter their decision-making through the lens of the Atkins diet. Have you ever tried to make a life-change based on a quick-fix mentality? What was the result?

2. Have you ever been the victim of identity theft through online hacking? What did the hacker purchase? How did you feel?
3. Which social media platforms cause you to stumble into the fear of missing out? Can you relate to Cherie's experience of setting unrealistic expectations based on what you've seen or heard online?
4. How does the prediction that three out of every eight years will be spent online change your thinking toward checking your phone?
5. What makes the combination of FOMO and parenting so difficult? How can you cope when it comes to facing the fears that you might not be able to provide every experience and item for your child? Are you a part of a group that encourages you as a parent? Begin the search for one if you're not.

Fostering Financial Foreplay

- List three action steps you can take to avoid your biggest FOMO triggers and take those steps.
- Pause each time you feel compelled to open up a social media feed this week and instead pray with gratitude for your spouse and thank God for providing your needs, listing the specifics.

CHAPTER 9

Who's the Center of Your Marriage?

From Consumer Connection to Christ-Centered Connection

My faith teaches me that the path to join souls in love must of necessity involve a crucifixion, and I think there's a metaphor in there for marriage.

DONALD MILLER

A long time ago in a galaxy far, far away, our grandparents used to buy chocolates in a big golden box. On top of the treasured treats lay a long, crinkly piece of black paper that made a satisfying sound when you squeezed it between your thumb and index finger. And beneath that layer of precious protection, the most delicious morsels were nestled down in their designated space of plastic casing. The trickiest part of choosing a chocolate lay in not knowing what was inside. Each was filled with a gooey flavor, but unless you remembered the specific shape of the delicacy from past experience, you'd end up choosing unwisely. As you puckered your face in disappointment, you may have been one of the confounding few who placed the half-eaten treat back in its little plastic home (gross bro, just throw it away).

In the decades since our grandparents purchased these boxed chocolates, candy packaging technology has improved in great strides. Many now include a treasure map indicating which particular sweet dwells in each micro-compartment. No longer do we have to endure a sickly-sweet center that's not to our liking. Instead, we can pick and choose exactly which flavors we want to savor.

The center of each candy used to wreck or complete the candy-eating experience. Whether a tart fruit or a smooth caramel, satisfaction or disappointment hinged on what rested in the middle. Hidden by a shell that looked exactly like every other one in the box, the inner taste determined the entire direction of the experience. The center of anything drives the experience.

While tasty candy isn't a complete metaphor for relationships, we all need to ask the crucial question, "What's at the center of our marriage?" Advertising and culture cry out to us about what we *need* as a married couple: Date nights! A new car! Jewelry! A weekend away! A new house! Children! A retreat, a vacation, a cruise! As individuals and as a couple, we're compelled to consume as much as possible, as quickly as possible, for as long as possible.

But in the end, buying stuff won't bring fulfillment. You can never own enough to fill the hole in your soul shaped only for God. Collecting more toys doesn't lead to everlasting life or even a full life on earth. Stuffing things where only the Spirit can go always disappoints. Our marriages fail when centered on consuming. Placing our faith in "things" instead of Jesus leaves us with a shaky foundation certain to wobble and crumble when life gets hard. Just like those mystery candies, the center drives the experience of our marriages. If our center is anything but Jesus, we'll find reasons to believe our lives aren't good enough. We'll be tempted to place our marriages back half-eaten in the metaphorical gold box and choose another piece. Then we'll repeat the cycle again and again. With nothing but an inedible box and a sour stomach, we're left empty and sad. *Consumerism always leads to enslavement. Only centering our lives on Jesus sets us free.*

But how do we pull our fingers back from the candy box? More often than not, we fall into patterns of purchasing things to fill the holes in our souls without even realizing what's going on. Moving our marriages from a consumer connection to a Christ-centered connection requires effort and intentionality, liberating us from bondage.

Renew Your Collective Mind: Brian

Locked in the back of a police cruiser, my mind scurried and analyzed the chances for escape. While I am sure the Dukes of Hazzard could have figured a way out, they had more experience than me. My predicament resembled Barney Fife more than Bo Duke. Occasionally, Barney, distracted by cleaning or whistling, would inadvertently lock himself in a jail cell. With some assistance, my similar confinement happened due to distraction as opposed to being in trouble with the law.

My college degree required a law enforcement internship. The detective I interned with allowed me to tag along with him and a school counselor to a conference where they were scheduled to speak. I declined shotgun and rode in the back of the cruiser for the first (and last) time. Upon reaching the conference center, the detective and the counselor talked through their presentation as they walked inside. I, on the other hand, got distracted by my ice cream cone and then couldn't exit the vehicle. Because . . . police cruiser. The rear doors do not open from the inside for good reason. It wasn't hot and I had ice cream, so I waited. Fortunately, the detective was, well, a detective and noticed the decreased head count. The ordeal lasted long enough for him to walk into the conference center and immediately walk back out and unlock me.

If you've ever felt trapped in a situation, even if it's temporary, you know the accompanying angst. Police cruisers aren't the only way we accidentally find ourselves trapped. When we become distracted or fall into the same unhealthy spending habits and routines common to those around us, our financial imprisonment lasts much longer than it takes to eat an ice cream cone. If we don't pay attention, our marriages sink in drain-circling patterns with no foreseeable escape. There is, however, a way to break free other than begging Otis the town drunk to hand you a key.

"Do not conform to the pattern of this world, but be transformed by the renewing of your mind. Then you will be able to test and approve what God's will is—his good, pleasing and perfect will" (Romans 12:2). The pattern of this world etches consumerism deep into our souls. Scarred by commerce and exhausted from chasing after more, better, newer, and faster, your marriage collapses. With your energies depleted by this never-ending unwinnable race, you shortchange your spouse the attention and affection they deserve.

You never planned disengagement from your husband or wife, so with good intentions you vow to reconnect. Sadly, the only pattern you know repeats and worsens your calamity. More money and better stuff cannot rectify a predicament produced by seeking more money and better stuff.

When heeded, God's admonishment against conforming to the pattern of this world protects you from disintegrating your marriage. The bigger house, the faster car, the better vacation, the next promotion, the trendier clothes, the wilder parties all lead toward dissatisfaction with your spouse, destruction in your finances, and dismantling your marriage. A constant yearning for new misappropriates your mind into desiring a different companion.

Erasing detrimental patterns necessitates complete transformation. The word *transformation* in the Greek (*metamorphose*) is where the word *metamorphosis* originates and is sometimes translated as "transfiguration." Through metamorphosis, a common caterpillar forms a chrysalis and later bursts out as a beautiful butterfly. This type of transformer differs from the Optimus Prime variety, because you can still kinda tell he's a truck. Transformation results in something unrecognizable from the original. But much like those fascinating robots, true transformation is more than meets the eye.

Reversing ingrained unhealthy patterns mimics resurrection. There is a death to the old way and a rebirth to new creation. A heart-change manifests and so does notable behavioral differentiation. God intervenes and molds us from broken to beautiful through the renewing of our minds. In our marriages, the collective renewal of our minds breaks harmful patterns. Husbands and wives resuscitate their marriage simply by breathing life into each other through Scripture. Reading the Bible together connects not only your minds but your hearts in a way that redirects your marriage to a better path. Learning and receiving God's Word together opens you up to a Christ-centered connection. Intentional, consistent time together discovering God's plan for your lives is the antithesis to consumerist patterns.

From a practical perspective, as you are reading God's Word together, you refrain from harmful patterns at least for that period of time. From a spiritual perspective, you form a Christ-centered connection that reorients both of your thinking. Consumerism stands no chance against the intimacy stimulated by renewing your minds together.

Saying Goodbye to Drexel: Cherie

When we moved into our house fifteen years ago, we didn't know we had hit the neighbor jackpot. On one side of our 1950s brick-and-stone ranch lived Gene and Cher, wonderful people who, thanks to their two dogs, have kept us from needing to buy our daughters pets. And on the other side lived Nettie and Drexel Martin, the sweetest, soft-talkingest people I have ever met. Drexel built their 1950s home with his own two hands.

All three households dwell on approximately an acre and a half of property. Part hobby and part habit, Drexel seemed to mow the yard every single day. Their neatly trimmed lawn tended to make ours look like an abandoned lot. Within the first couple of months of living there, I got our riding lawn mower stuck on a steep incline. Nettie and Drexel popped out their front door without hesitation and together pushed me out of the ditch. Did I mention they were in their late seventies at the time?

Over the years the Martins served as surrogate great-grandparents for both of our girls. They let them watch SpongeBob on their cable TV, poked them full of sugary snacks, and listened to countless hours of little girl stories. We're guessing they learned way more than necessary about our household through those afternoons spent entertaining the Lowe girls.

A couple years ago Drexel began mowing fewer and fewer days during the summer months. And we didn't see him driving golf balls in the backyard or walking the property in the early morning hours. His health declined and he spent time in and out of the hospital. We found it difficult to believe when hospice workers arrived in the driveway next door to begin guiding our sweet neighbor through his last days of life on earth. Our youngest daughter, Zoe, who was seven at the time, went over to Hula-Hoop in the front yard, hoping to bring a smile to his face as he laid in the hospital bed facing the front window.

It wasn't long before we found ourselves in the funeral home, hugging Nettie tightly and listening to the sweet sounds of the southern gospel music Drexel had loved his whole life long. Nettie spoke in her usual gentle tone.

"I just can't believe it, hon. I can't believe I've lost my buddy." Sixty-nine years had passed since they first pledged their wedding vows and Drexel, the love of her life, wouldn't mow the yard anymore, or play the guitar for short next-door visitors, or hold her hand as he and Nettie walked through the mall. Standing close to Nettie, I knew her life would never be the same without her sweet, kind-eyed Drexel. Seven decades of living together and loving each other leaves imprints on a soul.

Thanks to a number of long afternoon conversations I previously had while visiting with Nettie, I knew she and Drexel centered their marriage around Jesus. As I prayed my girls wouldn't break the beautiful porcelain figurines sprinkled around their living room, I glanced at the large Bible opened wide on a stand placed with prominence next to Nettie's chair. We talked about church and Drexel's role as an usher. More than once, the Gaithers—an Indiana-based southern gospel family—came up.

Drexel and Nettie worked hard and lived simply. Once, Brian asked Drexel if he could borrow an air pump. Noting the shiny, pristine condition of the tool, Brian asked, "Where did you get this, Drexel?" His reply: "I've had it since World War II." In the same house, with the same tools, and quality but not flashy vehicles, Nettie and Drexel built their marriage on something much more solid than what could be consumed. They built their marriage on a foundation of faith, a connection to Christ.

This is the endgame I long for in my own marriage. After all, someday my children will be tasked with cleaning up what I've left behind—the collection of Wonder Woman T-shirts, the home decor, the glass water bottles, my antique typewriter, my vintage-style bicycle—because I cannot take those things with me beyond this world. None of us can. All of the cute shoes, the perfect rug, the long sought-after wall art, the televisions, the cars, the purses, the beauty products, the furniture—none of it is eternal.

But here the majority of us sit, in the middle of suburbia, dreaming about that next "thing" we can get on sale, jonesing for our Amazon order to arrive. Stuff never satisfies. Stuff only causes us to long for more stuff. Our souls long to worship a Creator, but again and again we keep trying to find divine contentment in the created. It's a fruitless cycle where we mindlessly and desperately grab for anything and everything that might fill the gaping hole in our soul.

We occasionally do the same thing in our marriages too. We mislead ourselves into thinking a new house or a date night or a vacation or a swimming pool just might be the key to bringing us closer together. If only we could purchase that one magic item, maybe our problems would dissipate. Maybe we'd stop fighting and we would finally have the relationship we've always dreamed of. The lie repeats in our heads, deceiving our souls into thinking marriage can be bought, just like the other shiny items we want.

It's a cunning lie too. Because no one dares speak its ridiculousness out loud. I've never met anyone who said, "Our marriage is finally on the right track. We just bought a new camper!" or "We've finally gotten through that rough patch thanks to the new antique mirror I found on eBay."

Witnessing Nettie grieve Drexel shoved the truth into the forefront of my mind: You can't center your marriage on stuff. Stuff withers, expires, and goes out of style. Stuff is temporary. When the things you own are placed in the center of your relationship, everything tumbles down in an avalanche of household goods, electronics, clothes, and sporting equipment. All you have left is a pile of junk in the middle of your living room floor. You need more than stuff. You were made for more than stuff.

You were made for freedom.

In Galatians 5:13–15 (MSG), we learn what to do with the free life God calls us to:

> It is absolutely clear that God has called you to a free life. Just make sure that you don't use this freedom as an excuse to do whatever you want to do and destroy your freedom. Rather, use your freedom to serve one another in love; that's how freedom grows. For everything we know about God's Word is summed up in a single sentence: Love others as you love yourself. That's an act of true freedom. If you bite and ravage each

> other, watch out—in no time at all you will be annihilating each other, and where will your precious freedom be then?

You see, the pursuit of buying more and more only leads to never having enough. It's a prison, the furthest thing from freedom. But the key that unlocks a life and a marriage deceived into thinking you don't have enough? Serving one another in love. Let that sink in for a minute. *The only way you can truly be free from the soul-sickening cycle of consumerism is to love others as you love yourself.* You are called to love your spouse and serve your spouse. Within your marriage, that's how freedom grows.

Freedom vanishes when we begin to snip and snipe at each other. Unfortunately, our arguments over money escalate when we've caught the consumerism bug, purchasing items we haven't discussed or allowing our hearts to be captured by the pursuit of something new and improved that we just must have.

I have lots of dreams for our marriage. For starters, I'd like to remain married. While I'm not looking forward to that whole "death do us part" bit, if we can live lives centered on Jesus, I know that, like Nettie, I'll be okay. I dream that together we'll be able to use the money we've earned to bless and encourage men and women around the world who need the love of God in their lives. I dream we can be a part of changing our community and world in ways that bring forth redemption and beauty. I dream we'll witness our girls finding success and happiness, meaning and purpose in their lives. I dream we'll one day be able to travel together, experiencing the great wonders of God's creation.

I don't dream of annihilating Brian or our marriage.

When we place our aims on consuming, the endgame is annihilation. Centered on Christ, freedom to love grows. What's your dream?

Dream Big: Brian

Possibly the most egregious economic and marital error I committed happened two years prior to starting our debt-slaying journey. Burdened by fear, my fiscal mindset shifted and I approached Cherie with a program to tighten our belts and tackle our bills. In retrospect, it was more of an ambush than an approach. Without warning and with the gracefulness of a bull in a china shop, my authoritative pitch failed. My husbandly and financial failure was that my plan lacked any shred of love or empathy. Remember, "Husbands, love your wives, just as Christ loved the church" (Ephesians 5:25).

Structurally, the plan I accosted Cherie with was sound. The delivery, on the other hand, doomed what was a great concept. I served filet mignon on a toilet seat.

Brian: Cherie, we're going to totally redo our finances. I want to do this.

Cherie: (blank-faced, confused stare)

Brian begins to explain. Cherie begins to protest.

End scene in awkward silence.

The more nuanced mistake involved the misconception that the first step toward financial wellness is a plan. My hyperfocus on the methodology overrated the urgency for a strategy and neglected a critical element of financial change: a shared goal. By God's grace we course-corrected together and two years later charged toward the debt dragon's vanquish.

Paying off an insurmountable amount of debt did not begin with a plan, a budget, or even an agreement. Instead, our journey to financial freedom began with a shared dream. Rattled and disoriented by self-inflicted oppression in the form of ever-increasing payments, dreaming together catalyzed our resolve and oriented our trajectory.

While floundering in financial strain, letting life happen to you is easy but treacherous. When you live based on consumption, your marriage gets consumed by a never-ending pursuit of buying without purpose.

Dreaming together imagines a marriage where your Christ-centered connection dictates your future. Cherie and I dreamed about what our finances would look like if we didn't owe anyone any money. What could we do? We talked about which individuals and which organizations we could give more money. Who would we bless? We hoped for a method to manage our money in a way that impacted the kingdom of God. How would God show up? We envisioned providing a college education and a future for our kids. We dreamed about retiring early. We planned potential family vacations and getaways for just the two of us. We imagined a future where we weren't constantly stressed out about our lack of money or worrying if we could make ends meet. Would our world change? Our dreaming and God's faithfulness led to our deliverance.

Yes, a plan followed. But first, there was a dream.

Too often we zone in on the steps required to clean up our mess. We want a program or a process or a magic mathematical formula when what we really need is a shared dream. Absent a compelling reason for improvement, money misfires persist and consumerism creeps back into the picture. Align your hearts and resources around a unified Christ-centered purpose. Yes, you will need a plan, but a flow chart won't encourage you through difficult times the same way a clear dream will. Your plans, your budgets, and your short-term steps are designed around and because of your shared dreams. The dream always comes first. And a shared dream centered around Jesus eviscerates consumerism.

Adopting shared dreams feels unnatural at first. Asking each other these probing questions facilitates an honest discussion.

- What does a brighter financial future look like?
- What goals for our marriage, our family, and our community resonate with you?
- If our future selves wrote us a letter, what would our future selves ask us to do?
- What breaks your heart?
- What makes your heart sing?
- What are we doing now that will help us realize our shared dreams?
- What do we need to stop doing to help us realize our shared dreams?
- Do our shared dreams align with God's will for our lives?

The Difference between a Good and a Great Marriage: Cherie

I'm pretty sure I wouldn't remember anything about my life or the early years of parenting if it weren't for the Facebook Memories function. I do a decent job of recording the special moments of our lives online so the grandparents and friends sprinkled across the globe can know what's going on with our family. But ask me to recall a specific memory in recent years, and I find myself struggling. Thanks, technology; you're swell!

As an added bonus, in the mix of baby photos and silly expressions from my kids, I often find bits and pieces of song lyrics, quotes from podcasts, Scripture references, and passages from books I was reading at the time. A few weeks ago I stumbled across these words on a status update I shared without a reference to the source. I'm not sure if it was a mentor, friend, or an author, but the sentiment is too powerful not to quote here: "Somebody recently told me that the difference between a good marriage and a great marriage are the two or three things you don't say every day."

The longer I'm married, the more I feel this wisdom in my bones. Most days, I would benefit (and, as a result, our marriage would benefit) if I learned how to keep my "moves faster than my brain" mouth shut. Don't get me wrong, there's a time and a place to be bold with your spouse and share difficult truth. Within the context of marriage, we refine one another by pointing out the ways we all fall short of God's plan for our lives. However, I'm pretty sure gasping when my husband makes what I would consider to be a less than preferable lane change on the interstate does little to make him look more like Jesus. It does on the other hand make him irritable with me while simultaneously eating away at our marriage.

We all long for great marriages. Great marriages necessitate work and grit. They demand serving in love and adjusting our expectations. Great marriages ignore what culture says we need or deserve and instead choose a much more challenging path of placing our spouse's needs in front of our own. Fueled by marketing frenzy, we ingrain our souls with messages like "You can have it all" or "Have it your way."

Friends, we can't have it all, and it can't always be our way, not if we want to remain married at least. In matrimony, you're not a doormat, but you can't be a bulldozer either. Instead, you must replace selfish desires with love.

Raise your hand if you heard 1 Corinthians 13 at a wedding. It's a great passage of Scripture, but the repetition sometimes causes us to miss its deep meaning. We may even mumble through the words absentmindedly and never take them into our hearts.

A wise friend of mine pointed out that maybe I should approach this passage with new eyes. Especially in the context of marriage, she said I should consider replacing the word *love* with my own name in each of the verses . . .

Cherie is patient, Cherie is kind.

She does not envy, she does not boast, she is not proud.

She does not dishonor others, she is not self-seeking, she is not easily angered, she keeps no record of wrongs.

Cherie does not delight in evil but rejoices with the truth. She always protects, always trusts, always hopes, always perseveres.

Ouch. My ego thoroughly checked, I began to see my own failings in a slow-motion replay. Each instance of violating God's aim for my life rolled through my brain in high-definition clarity. If I'm honest about my own sin, I rarely fit any of the descriptors in this iconic love passage. Reading the words in print right now stings. I ache in my awareness of complete, utter lack of love in my life.

But we would all be exhausted by the mandates of love if we had to do it through our own strength. Living lives of love is impossible without the grace and strength that come only from God. Thriving, healthy marriages devoid of God's love are rare or nonexistent. What does love have to do with consumerism, you may ask. Love requires us to die to our own selfish desires in pursuit of something much greater. When we say no to ourselves, we begin to look a little bit more like Jesus.

I love the quote at the beginning of this chapter. I'll share it again in case you missed it: "My faith teaches me that the path to join souls in love must of necessity involve a crucifixion, and I think there's a metaphor in there for marriage."[1]

When souls join, something must die to create a new life together. Sometimes that death is painful. It's never without sacrifice. And sometimes, the other individual doesn't choose the same path of crucifixion. Maybe one spouse decides to pursue stuff, potentially leaving the other spouse out in the cold all alone. But often, the choice is much more subtle and seductive. It's tempting to think all the purchases we make are necessary and all the purchases our spouse makes are frivolous. Our natural bent toward self deceives us into thinking only one of us makes sacrifices and "it's always me."

Even if you're right in your assumption, it doesn't mean you should fire back and make selfish choices yourself. Retaliatory spending only compounds the money struggles couples carry.

It's not popular or trendy to say you need to die to yourself daily in your marriage. It's certainly not a picture of "finding your bliss" or living a carefree life. A countercultural commitment like this smacks of daring and danger. You risk without the promise of reward or even a potential requital. But then again, Jesus didn't die for us while we were dying for Him. He went first. There was no guarantee we would respond to His act of love. There was no action on our part or even a promise. He laid down His life because it was the only way for our souls to join with His.

We've seen couples perform miraculous acts of love for their husbands and wives, laying down their own desires and dreams to reflect Jesus. Holding a hand during chemotherapy, standing vigil by a hospital bed, giving up a career for the benefit of the other, staying married and fighting for their relationship even after heartrending infidelity, moving thousands of miles away so the other could be closer to aging parents, sharing the grief and challenge of infertility—in moments like these we breathe prayers of "Only Jesus could help someone make a choice like this. Thank You, God."

We probably all center our thinking on these sorts of momentous sacrifices. But any time you choose to give up what you want for the life-giving benefit of another, you're reflecting a Christ-centered connection. It may look much more modest: brewing the coffee, balancing the checkbook, taking out the trash, providing a moment of respite after a long day, packing a lunch, firing up the lawnmower, or simply staring into his or her eyes and saying, "I love you." Maybe it's writing him an encouraging note. Maybe it's sincerely listening to what she has to say. Maybe it's showing up for what matters to the other. If it's important to them, it's important to you. The day-to-day, nonglamorous opportunities abound. Whether you choose to take advantage of them is up to you.

I'm not saying dying to our own way or even dying to consumerism is easy. It can be agony. But when we vow to join our lives and our souls together, it's the deal we make. Christ-centered marriage isn't for sissies. Don't get me wrong, love between two committed Christ followers reenacts God's love for us. It's a thing of divine beauty. Crucifying love—love that dies to self and brings your spouse closer to God—is the difference between a good marriage and a great marriage.

Escaping Quicksand

Growing up in the 80s, it seemed like every TV show or movie we watched featured at least one scene where a character got caught in quicksand. If you were a kid in this era, you anticipated finding quicksand on a vacation to the beach or simply in your own backyard. Adulthood revealed much less physical quicksand in our lives, but probably more metaphorical quicksand than we ever anticipated.

Consumerism sneaks in like quicksand. Before we know it, we're up to our necks in debt, wildly grasping for something to pull us out of a hole of our own making. It's easy to pull down someone else into the same mess or be pulled in as a casualty ourselves. As married couples we need to be on the watch for the traps of consumerism.

The remedy to consumerism is love, specifically the sacrificial love of Jesus. Serving in love and dying to ourselves reflects Jesus. Love and laying down our desires causes freedom to grow. We don't have to be locked away in the prison of consumerism. We can have great marriages centered on Christ's love. Which in the end tastes far better than even the best chocolate in the gold box.

Discussion Questions

1. What's in the center of your favorite candies? Have you ever tasted something you thought would have a different flavor?
2. Brian said, "God intervenes and molds us from broken to beautiful through the renewing of our minds." Why is it important for us to renew our minds together as married couples? In what ways are you renewing your minds together? What methods of renewing your minds could you add?
3. In what areas of your marriage or life have you seen freedom grow as a result of serving through love?
4. How can the dreams we have for our future fuel the plan we make for our money together?
5. Centering your marriage on Christ requires death to self. Where have you seen culture depict a happy marriage—commercials, sitcoms, movies, books?

How is this different from or similar to a Christ-centered marriage?

Fostering Financial Foreplay

- Write out the love passage from 1 Corinthians 13 on an index card, replacing the word *love* with your own name. Pray over the uniquely personalized Scripture, asking God to help you exemplify His love to your spouse beginning today. Now, trade cards with your spouse and pray over their life.
- Have your own dream date night. Plan an evening to discuss your dreams as a couple. Use the questions Brian listed in this chapter (p. 196) to shape your thinking. Create a visual to put on the refrigerator or a dream board to hang on the wall. Draw pictures of your envisioned future, print out graphics from the internet, or simply handwrite your shared dreams. Place the visual in a space you both regularly pass, to be reminded of what matters most.
- This week, look for opportunities to put your spouse first. Journal the ways you witness freedom growing from those acts of love.
- Take a twenty-minute time out with your spouse. Share with each other the ways you're grateful he or she has put you first.

CHAPTER 10

Begin Again

From Old Ways of Thinking to New Beginnings

Because it is the nature of love to create, a marriage itself is something which has to be created, so that, together we become a new creature.

MADELEINE L'ENGLE

Our origin story began with what Brian referred to as the best directions he ever received. But part of our origin story involved ignoring directions altogether. Months into our relationship, on Cherie's October birthday weekend, she came home from college to spend a fun-filled time with the young man she would marry the following year. We planned trips to explore a pumpkin patch and hike a National Forest. The changing colors of the leaves in Indiana light up the autumn sky, and we wanted to experience this beauty together.

Our weekend together started with disappointment. We arrived at the well-hyped pumpkin patch only to discover it was closed. As young idealists, we had no back-up plan. Instead of a creative and fun evening making memories together, we played our first game of "I dunno, what do you want to do?" as a couple.

The following day, determined to recover from the smashing pumpkin dreams of the night before, we gathered snacks for our first short road trip together. Excited and optimistic, we chatted about our school lives, our passions, our hopes, and our aspirations. Our conversation never lulled. After two or so hours on the highway, as we selected a new CD (a round, shiny, circular disc that in ancient times stored music), one of us noticed the flashing red and blue lights of a state trooper in the rearview mirror. That's right, one of our early dates involved a police officer as an unfortunate third wheel. Apparently, in the excitement of each other's company, we gazed more at each other than the speedometer.

Maybe it was mercy for our stupidity or appreciation for our young love, but the officer declined to issue a ticket. As the officer sent us on our way, we thanked him and asked, "How close are we to Hoosier National Forest?" The sullen officer suddenly grinned and replied, "You're not."

Wait, we've been on the road for a long time, how are we not on the fringes of fall glory? Surely the officer who travels these highways for a living must be mistaken. We pulled into the next town, a quaint berg called Orleans, with a population of two thousand, to ask for directions (something you did before smartphones and GPS). Since all other businesses were closed, we darted into a small knick-knack shop to avoid the now impending thunderstorm. The owner greeted us, grinned (perhaps she was related to the officer), and explained we were over sixty miles away from our intended destination. Under no circumstances was Orleans on the way to Hoosier National Forest unless of course you lived in Orleans, Indiana. We were lost.

Let's recap: closed pumpkin patch, detained by law enforcement, drifted off course from our destination, torrential downpour. This relationship could have ended on the long (probably quiet) ride home. But it didn't. We weren't fazed. We grabbed hands and ran across the rain-soaked street to a gazebo on the town square. We held each other and we danced. To no music, we danced. Our relationship didn't end in Orleans; it began there.

When we were lost in our finances, we held on to one another. When we experienced the storms of life, we held on to one another. Early in our relationship we discovered that it doesn't matter where you are going; it matters who you are with.

Right now, if you feel lost when it comes to your money and your marriage, what matters most is who you are with—your spouse. Life doesn't always go as planned. The curves and bumps along the way might bruise us, but there's opportunity for romance even amid tumult, and smart finance can spring from mistakes too. Don't let feelings of defeat derail your efforts. Begin again by shifting your old ways of thinking into new and hopeful beginnings.

Your marriage is not over; your financial situation not beyond repair. In fact, you have everything you need today to kiss the old story goodbye and start walking toward the horizon of a new beginning.

Lessons in Hydration: Brian

My thirteen-year-old nephew accompanied me as road support on one of Cherie's 160-mile bike rides. The day before the ride, I got a call from my friend Mike. "Hey, Brian, my buddy and I are doing this ride and don't have road support. If we get in a jam, can I call you?"

"Absolutely."

Mike had been in my community group for years, and I knew he trained hard for this event. It wouldn't hinder my road support for Cherie, so I wasn't going to let him down.

My nephew and I saw Cherie and her crew off and proceeded to meet them at designated stops. The ride occurs every July and that particular year, it was scorching hot. At the lunch stop, I saw Mike. "Man, you look great!" I cheered. Mike's buddy, sitting on the ground resting, asked, "How do I look?"

"Well, I've never seen you before, but you look like crap. You don't look good at all." Everybody laughed. To this day, I don't think they thought I was serious.

After a pit stop with Cherie's group around the 110-mile mark, my nephew and I headed back on the road and I got a call from Mike. "My buddy's not going to make it, but I think I've got enough left to finish. We saw you just pass us. Can you pick him up?"

"Absolutely."

We doubled back and proceeded to pick up a complete stranger. He looked worse than before. A lot worse. I was already plotting how I would explain a dead body in the back of the car. What ensued next was an exchange I will never forget.

First, I went to lift his bike onto the bike rack. I couldn't lift it. A road bike is light—lift it over your head with one hand light. So I used two hands. Nope. Whatever lead this bike was made of required me to bend my knees in a full-on Olympic squat press. I also noticed his pedals didn't have cages or clips. Cages or clips allow riders to use both sides of their legs—the quadriceps to push the pedal down and the hamstrings to lift through the back half of the pedal stroke. Mike's buddy was using twice the energy necessary to propel a Sherman Tank of a bicycle 110 miles in the flaming heat of July. Upon further inquiry, he was a marathoner who couldn't understand why he was spent. He had purchased the first bike he saw at a local big-box retailer.

Here's where the conversation got interesting:

Me: "I've got Gatorade, water, and bananas. You're probably dehydrated."

Mike's buddy: "I don't think so. No, thanks. I'm fine."

Me: "Okay. But I think you're dehydrated."

Mike's buddy: "I don't think so . . . I really started to cramp up out there."

Me: "You're dehydrated."

Mike's buddy: "I don't think so . . . It was weird earlier. I tried to go to the bathroom and couldn't."

Me: "You're dehydrated."

Mike's buddy: "I don't think so . . . Riding takes it out of you. I don't get this lightheaded when I do a marathon."

Me: "You're dehydrated."

Thirteen-year-old nephew: [covers face in hands, shakes head]

We reached the parking lot which was a short jog from the finish line and got out of the car. Sorta. Mike's buddy really didn't make it out of the car the way humans usually do. He more fell out of the car than stepped out of the car—onto his back with his legs bent up in the fetal position.

Exasperated, I straddled my feet over each side of his stiffened carcass, drew close to his face, and spoke slowly but loudly, "You're dehydrated!" We jammed a banana and a Gatorade in his face and left him there to nibble his banana like a baby chimpanzee. We wanted to see Cherie finish.

Mike's buddy was a great guy and a fine athlete. The truth is that none of us know when we're dehydrated. That may be one of the symptoms. We can just as easily get dehydrated in our money and our marriages. Stay well hydrated by taking steps ahead of time. Let's look at some of Mike's buddy's mistakes and how you can avoid them.

You're carrying too much weight. His bike was way too heavy. Maybe you bring work stress home and it carries over into your relationship. Maybe the clutches of debt are squeezing you and holding you down. Maybe you've suffered the soul-crushing trauma of losing a child, endured a housefire, or received a terrible diagnosis. Lighten your load by casting your burdens on the shoulders of our Savior. Reach out to your community for help carrying the weight.

You haven't invested in the right equipment. He didn't have cages or clips. Read a marriage book. Go to a seminar together or on a retreat specifically geared toward improving your marriage, your communication, or your money. Do a career evaluation and assess what tools you need to obtain a less stifling vocation. Invest in software or other financial resources to aid in the management of your money.

You haven't trained because you were confident in your other abilities. He was a marathoner, not a biker. So what if you run a successful landscaping business or you're an ER nurse? The skills are transferable, but not the same. When you make your marriage a priority, you do all you can to train for that relationship. Learn what you need to know about your spouse and expend the time necessary to take care of the person you've pledged your life to.

You're not listening to wisdom around you. He wasn't listening to my assessment of his physical condition. Internet trolls will say harsh things. But when you've asked for feedback from a trusted source and the response is "You look like crap and may be dehydrated"—listen. Take action. Be mentored. Seek wise counsel and advice. Don't be afraid to go to marriage or financial counseling.

You're dehydrated. He was dehydrated! Drink from the only source that will quench your thirst: Jesus. The thing about hydrating is that you have to do it daily. Put your spouse in a position to avoid dehydration too, but don't *ever* say: "You look like crap."

Calm in the Chaos: Cherie

My most amazing teacher was my first. My mom spent well over two decades of her life inspiring students in the classroom and encouraging colleagues pursuing excellence in education. She also spent forty-plus years as a parent guiding sometimes less-than-eager pupils. Her ability to break complex problems into small and manageable parts came in handy when I felt overwhelmed by a paper or Algebra equation. Her random facts and corny puns caused my teenage self to develop an eye-rolling ability at a world-champion level. Good news! I've inherited her skill set and now my kids benefit from flexible eye muscles too.

Do you want to know where my mom's teaching gifts came most alive? In the vacation Bible school classroom. The small rural church where I grew up boasted a lively Bible school crowd one week of the year every summer. It was a magical place where Hydrox cookies on white napkins greeted us in the snack area because the budget couldn't afford real Oreos. And in the sanctuary, the pianist, Joyce, plunked out "Hallelu-, hallelu-, hallelu-, hallelujah" for kids squirming on one side of the pews, immediately followed by the equally sugar-fueled counterpart located on the opposite side of the aisle, ~~screaming~~ singing "Praise ye the Lord!" Crafts weren't made from yarn and paper. Oh, no. We got to use real hammers and nails, baby. It was a week of sheer on-the-edge adventure for young Cherie.

For the many highs of VBS, your experience hinged on the volunteer staff when it came to actual classroom time. You could end up in a snorefest class where the Bible was taught by an octogenarian who didn't like kids. But if you were oh-so-lucky, you landed in my mom's class. When it came to VBS, my mom pulled out all the stops to bring Scripture alive.

There was the year when she constructed an enormous cluster of grapes from a stick and purple balloons to illustrate Joshua and Caleb's spy mission into Canaan in Numbers 13. When we learned about manna and quail falling from the sky in Exodus 16, she cooked pheasants (close enough) and baked a sweet wafer bread for us to eat. But the year she taught about Jesus and His disciples was the best year of all.

In the center of her classroom, my mom had a man from the church place his well-loved fishing boat. It was far from an authentic Galilean sailing vessel, given that we lived in the Midwest. But as Mom told stories from the Gospels, all the kids squeezed onto the wooden seats, listening with rapt attention. We could almost smell the water, feel the sea spray on our faces. We imagined Jesus (instead of a woman in skirted 1980s fashion) sharing deep truths and teaching life lessons. It wasn't so long ago and far away. Jesus was right there with us in the boat.

The experience never left my memory even though all but one of the stories did. I'm sure she talked about becoming fishers of people, Peter pulling a nearly bursting net of fish up from the lake, and walking on water. But the only specific lesson I can recall was the story of Jesus calming the storm.

Let me refresh your memory if it's been awhile since you've been to VBS too. Found in the books of Matthew, Mark, and Luke, our story begins with Jesus and His disciples going on an evening sea cruise. Mark 4:35–41 is probably my favorite retelling because it's rich with details. Mark and I both love the opportunity to overexplain. I'm biblical like that. Here's the original account of the events:

> That day when evening came, he said to his disciples, "Let us go over to the other side." Leaving the crowd behind, they took him along, just as he was, in the boat. There were also other boats with him. A furious squall came up, and the waves broke over the boat, so that it was nearly swamped. Jesus was in the stern, sleeping on a cushion. The disciples woke him and said to him, "Teacher, don't you care if we drown?"
>
> He got up, rebuked the wind and said to the waves, "Quiet! Be still!" Then the wind died down and it was completely calm.
>
> He said to his disciples, "Why are you so afraid? Do you still have no faith?" They were terrified and asked each other, "Who is this? Even the wind and the waves obey him!"

(A) Let's begin by noticing that Jesus and the disciples left the crowd behind. Maybe they felt overstimulated. Maybe they became aware of their need for hydration. Or maybe they knew the crowd wasn't traveling in the same direction they were. Whatever the reason, there was movement from one place to another.

(B) They weren't traveling alone. There were other boats there with them. Disciples of Jesus—the people who are seeking to learn what it means to look like Him—would be smart to travel in packs, or community.

(C) Jesus shares the ability to sleep through a terrifying storm with every other member of my family. If it starts sprinkling, I'm wide awake. Everyone else in this house could snooze straight through a forty-five-minute hailstorm of apocalyptic proportions and never even bat an eyelash. Also, Mark is the only author to point out the fact that Jesus is asleep on a cushion. I find this hilarious. "And there He was, just sawing logs, plopped down on an IKEA KLOTULLÖRT while the rest of us were fuh-reaking out in full-on panic mode."

(D) "Teacher, don't you care if we drown?" The disciples' first statement wasn't one of information: "Um, Jesus, just thought You might want to know it's raining." Or even a panicked plea for assistance, "Help, please!" It was a questioning of God's care. Hmmm . . . a good observation to ponder.

(E) Jesus takes care of business before He works on the hearts of His followers. He does what needs to be done (calms the storm) before asking why His disciples were afraid or noting their lack of faith.

(F) Last but not least, instead of saying thank you, the disciples talk amongst themselves in terror. It's easy to judge their behavior and think we'd do differently, but I think this is a common human response. We're slow to show gratitude, quick to return to fear.

So what does this have to do with your money and your marriage?

(A) You may need to leave the crowd. Jesus and His followers moved in a different direction from society. They weren't doing what everyone else was doing. If you want calm in your finances and peace in your marriage, move in the direction of Jesus, not the crowd.

(B) Leaving the crowd doesn't mean becoming the Lone Ranger. Your money and your marriage thrive in like-minded community. Attend a church, join a small group, find money mentors, sign up for a Bible study or course like Financial Peace University to develop the network you need.

(C) Rest is holy. Take a nap with your spouse. Power down your cell phone. Get away for the weekend. Rejuvenate.

(D) In case you were wondering, God cares about you. He cares about your money. He cares about your marriage. He cares about your finances. God cares about your future.

(E) Calming the storms of your money and your marriage involves trust. Sometimes heart changes don't come until after you begin to put one faithful foot in front of the other. Allow God to transform your mind while you're doing the work. Don't wait for the heart transformation to begin the work (or you may never get anywhere).

(F) Choose gratitude over fear. Say thank you to God often for His rescue, for His provision, for the gift of your spouse. Say thank you often to your spouse—for their sacrifice, for their kindness, for their love. Anytime you feel fear creeping in, shut it down with thankfulness.

Because the truth is, rain or shine, you're in this together. And that's a beautiful thing.

May You Be Found

Dear friends, thank you for taking this journey with us. We pray your hearts have been encouraged and spirits bolstered. Even though we may never meet face-to-face, we love you. We acknowledge we don't have all the answers when it comes to money and marriage and that we don't ever get it completely right. Developing financial foreplay is a process. For deepened intimacy and flourishing finances, we all have to be open to change and moving toward improvement.

For that reason, we long for you to continue to grow, change, open up, and communicate, to find strength, peace, and hope in the midst of your love.

Love is the most powerful force in the universe. Together and through love, you and your spouse will succeed with both your money and, more important, your marriage. Your affection and trust for one another will reach new heights as you grow together in love. With unparalleled wisdom, King Solomon best articulates the breadth of love's power. In Song of Songs, he pens these compelling and beautiful words:

> Hang my locket around your neck,
>   wear my ring on your finger.
> Love is invincible facing danger and death.
>   Passion laughs at the terrors of hell.
> The fire of love stops at nothing—
>   it sweeps everything before it.
> Flood waters can't drown love,
>   torrents of rain can't put it out.
> Love can't be bought, love can't be sold—
>   it's not to be found in the marketplace.
>
> **SONG OF SONGS 8:6–7 (MSG)**

The love you and your spouse share, more powerful than the forces of nature, can't be bought or sold. It stands in the face of fear—fear of failure, fear of the future, fear of your financial situation—and laughs. The love God has ordained between the two of you can't be stopped, quenched, or swept away. The love of your marriage endures.

May your love for one another be unquenchable, unstoppable, and invincible.

May your passion burn brightly, blissfully, and intensely.

May you live your vows each day, always keeping your promises.

May you always hold hands in the rain, kiss goodnight, and slow dance in your kitchen.

May you dream and chase big dreams together.

May your wallets, hearts, and legs intertwine in harmony.

May you always seek forgiveness.

May you always forgive.

May your marriage reflect God's sacrificial love for us.

May the financial barriers between you come tumbling down.

And may you always pursue smart finance and spicy romance.

Acknowledgments

We owe a deep debt of gratitude—the only type of debt we'll take on—to a number of people who influenced, encouraged, prayed over, and provided wisdom for this work.

Special thanks to Angela Scheff and the team at The Christopher Ferebee Agency. Thanks for keeping us on task, Angela. Your encouragement and support were indispensable at every stage of this project. You stuck with us, never let us down, and always exceeded our expectations. Forever we'll be grateful.

Hugs, high fives, and all the revisions in GIFs to Stephanie Smith, editor extraordinaire. Your tireless effort and unique insight brought out our best stories and helped form a much more cohesive, thoughtful work. You are a rock star.

To the Write Brilliant team that's more like family, especially Margaret Feinberg, Jonathan Merritt, Jessica Riche, and Leif Oines. Not only did you believe in us when we were uncertain of ourselves, but you also gave us the tools we needed to get the job done. We're over the moon thankful for you in more ways than we can number.

Beyond patient and longsuffering when we sat for hours writing and editing, our kids are a great gift. Anna and Zoe, you are our favorite works of art. Thank you for holding down the fort and making this book possible.

We are both blessed with "stand in the gap" parents—Gary and Patty Walters and Ron and Sally Lowe—who lent a helping hand during this project. Thank you for all you've done to encourage and support us as writers, a couple, and a family.

To the pastor A-Team—Scot, Danny, Ryan, Michael, Brodie, and Devin—once again you jumped in feetfirst with wisdom and prayer to undergird every step of the way. You make us want to load up the black and red van and go for another ride.

For more than a decade the LoweLife Community Group has provided comfort, encouragement, laughter, joy, learning, love, physical and emotional support, and a soft place to land for our souls. You are our people, the ones we can call in the middle of the night, no questions asked. Thank you for persisting and persevering with us. Love God. Love People. Show Up.

Many thanks to Majors Bob and Collette Webster and the wonderful people at Hidden Falls Salvation Army Camp for providing respite and a place to write many of the words in this book.

From Cherie: Thank you, Jackie, for being the type of friend who shows up three times a week so we can do burpees and box jumps (even on your birthday!). You've celebrated the highs and pushed me through the lows of writing this book. For the texts, the Wonder Woman swag, the hours spent walking and working out, I am undone with gratitude.

From Cherie: Julie King, you make my world a better place. For your wisdom, prayers, encouragement, willingness to carry heavy boxes, waving violently at me from the back of the room to wrap it up, truck driving skills, and so much more, I appreciate you more than you know.

We are grateful for the married couples who have poured into our lives for the past nineteen years—too many to list here. We love you, and your words and examples have changed our lives.

Deep gratitude for Team Zondervan: Brandon Henderson, Robin Barnett, Kim Tanner, and many more working behind the scenes to bring the best version of *Your Money, Your Marriage* to life and into as many hands as possible. Thank you from the bottom of our hearts.

Endnotes

Chapter 2

1. Taryn Hillin, "New Survey Sheds Light On What Married Couples Fight About Most," June 03, 2014. *The Huffington Post*, June 3, 2014, http://www.huffingtonpost.com/2014/06/03/marriage-finances_n_5441012.html.
2. Catherine Rampell, "Money Fights Predict Divorce Rates," *The New York Times*, December 07, 2009. https://economix.blogs.nytimes.com/2009/12/07/money-fights-predict-divorce-rates/.
3. Jeffrey Dew, Sonya Britt, and Sandra Huston, "Examining the Relationship Between Financial Issues and Divorce," *Family Relations*, 61, no. 4 (October 2012): 615–28, http://onlinelibrary.wiley.com/doi/10.1111/j.1741-3729.2012.00715.x/abstract.

Chapter 3

1. "TD Bank Love and Money 2015 Overview," *TD Bank News*, June 2015. https://mediaroom.tdbank.com/couplesoverview.
2. Paul Golden, "Financial Infidelity Poses Challenge for Couples," *National Endowment for Financial Education*, February 14, 2014, http://www.nefe.org/Press-Room/News/Financial-Infidelity-Poses-Challenge-for-Couples.
3. Seth Stephens-Davidowitz, "Searching for Sex," *The New York Times*, January 24, 2015, https://www.nytimes.com/2015/01/25/opinion/sunday/seth-stephens-davidowitz-searching-for-sex.html.

4. Heather Kelly, "The bizarre, lucrative world of 'unboxing' videos," *CNN*, February 13, 2014, http://www.cnn.com/2014/02/13/tech/web/youtube-unboxing-videos/index.html.
5. Jeff Thompson, "Is Nonverbal Communication a Numbers Game?" *Psychology Today*, September 30, 2011, https://www.psychologytoday.com/blog/beyond-words/201109/is-nonverbal-communication-numbers-game.
6. Truman Capote, *In Cold Blood: A True Account of Multiple Murder and Its Consequences* (New York: Modern Library, 2013), 105.
7. Lindsay Konsko, "Credit Cards Make You Spend More: Studies," NerdWallet, June 01, 2016, https://www.nerdwallet.com/blog/credit-cards/credit-cards-make-you-spend-more/.
8. https://www.goodreads.com/quotes/264270-as-i-grow-older-i-pay-less-attention-to-what

Chapter 4

1. Greg Smalley. "Focus on the Family: Do You and Your Spouse Handle Conflict Well?" Focus on the Family. February 11, 2016. https://www.facebook.com/focusonthefamily/photos/a.380277663519.157071.51405613519/10153503409723520/?type=3&theater.
2. Rorke Denver, "Calm Is Contagious." Leadercast. Accessed January 14, 2018. https://www.leadercast.com/programs/calm-is-contagious. In his inspiring words, Denver also declares, "Panic is contagious; chaos is contagious, stupid, 100% contagious." All great words for both leaders and married couples.

Chapter 5

1. Chip Heath and Dan Heath, *Switch: How to Change Things When Change Is Hard* (New York: Broadway Books, 2010), 93.
2. John Ortberg, "Ruthlessly Eliminate Hurry," *CT Pastors*, July 2002, http://www.christianitytoday.com/pastors/2002/july-online-only/cln20704.html.
3. Andy Stanley, "Brand New: What Love Requires," *North Point.*

February 22, 2015. http://northpoint.org/messages/brand-new/what-love-requires/.

4. Lindsay Holmes, "7 Reasons Why We Should Be Giving More Hugs," *The Huffington Post*, March 27, 2014, https://www.huffingtonpost.com/2014/03/27/health-benefits-of-huggin_n_5008616.html.
5. Rebecca Kessler, "Hugs Follow a 3-Second Rule," *Science*, July 28, 2011, http://www.sciencemag.org/news/2011/01/hugs-follow-3-second-rule.

Chapter 6

1. If you or someone you love is in an abusive relationship, go to www.thehotline.org or, since sometimes an abuser monitors computer usage, call the National Domestic Violence Hotline at 1-800-799-7233 (TTY 1-800-787-3224). You can also seek faith-based counseling referrals from Focus on the Family at 1-800-A-FAMILY.
2. Alain de Botton, "Why You Will Marry the Wrong Person," *The New York Times*, May 28, 2016, https://www.nytimes.com/2016/05/29/opinion/sunday/why-you-will-marry-the-wrong-person.html.
3. We first discovered this idea from Richard Rohr, "Living in Deep Time," interview by Krista Tippett, *On Being*, podcast audio, April 13, 2017, https://onbeing.org/programs/richard-rohr-living-in-deep-time-apr2017/. For a shorter eight-minute homily, listen to Richard Rohr, "God Is All Vulnerable More Than All Mighty," June 5, 2016, *Center for Action and Contemplation*, https://cac.org/god-vulnerable-mighty/.

Chapter 7

1. For a fascinating exploration of more than one study on physical writing versus digital record keeping, read Michael Grothaus, "This Is How the Way You Read Impacts Your Memory and Productivity," October 11, 2017. *Fast Company*, https://www

.fastcompany.com/40476984/this-is-how-the-way-you-read-impacts-your-memory-and-productivity.

2. In chapter 4 of *Slaying the Debt Dragon*, "Budgets Are Your Battle-Ax," Cherie spells out more specifics for giving, saving, and spending. On page 221, in the endnotes, you'll also find an exploration on how much you should be giving if you are also paying off debt. Cherie Lowe, *Slaying the Debt Dragon: How One Family Conquered Their Money Monster and Found an Inspired Happily Ever After* (Carol Stream, IL: Tyndale Momentum, 2014), 57–78, 221.
3. Kimberly Lankford, "Make a Date to Talk About Money This Valentine's Day," Kiplinger's Personal Finance, February 2005, 90.
4. A fantastic, comprehensive read on marriage and money can be found here: Kerri Anne Renzulli, "The Newlyweds' Guide to Financial Success," *Money*, June 1, 2017, http://time.com/money/4776640/money-tips-married-couples/.
5. Cherie Lowe, *Slaying the Debt Dragon: How One Family Conquered Their Money Monster and Found an Inspired Happily Ever After* (Carol Stream, IL: Tyndale Momentum, 2014), 57–78.
6. This article gives a thorough explanation of how the envelope system works: Rachel Cruze, "The Envelope System Explained," *Dave Ramsey*, https://www.daveramsey.com/blog/envelope-system-explained.
7. Lindsay Konsko, "Credit Cards Make You Spend More: Studies," *NerdWallet*, July 8, 2014, https://www.nerdwallet.com/blog/credit-cards/credit-cards-make-you-spend-more/.
8. Nelson D. Schwartz, "Credit Cards Encourage Extra Spending as the Cash Habit Fades Away," *New York Times*, March 25, 2016, https://www.nytimes.com/2016/03/27/your-money/credit-cards-encourages-extra-spending-as-the-cash-habit-fades-away.html.
9. "Partitioning," Behavioraleconomics.com, https://www.behavioraleconomics.com/mini-encyclopedia-of-be/partitioning/.
10. For more practical envelope strategies, see Cherie Lowe, *Slaying*

the Debt Dragon: How One Family Conquered Their Money Monster and Found an Inspired Happily Ever After (Carol Stream, IL: Tyndale Momentum, 2014), 73–75.

11. Nancy Fitzgerald, "Why your clutter is costing you a bundle," *MarketWatch*, April 11, 2017, accessed October 14, 2017, http://www.marketwatch.com/story/why-your-clutter-is-costing-you-a-bundle-2017-04-06.
12. Nancy Fitzgerald, "Why your clutter is costing you a bundle," *MarketWatch*, April 11, 2017, http://www.marketwatch.com/story/why-your-clutter-is-costing-you-a-bundle-2017-04-06.
13. Stan Berenstain and Jan Berenstain, *The Berenstain Bears Think of Those in Need* (New York: Random House, 1999).
14. Bernadette D. Proctor, Jessica L. Semega, and Melissa A. Kollar, "Income and Poverty in the United States: 2015," *United States Census Bureau*, September 13, 2016, https://www.census.gov/library/publications/2016/demo/p60-256.html.
15. Joshua Fields Millburn and Ryan Nicodemus, "Getting Rid of Just-in-Case Items: 20 Dollars, 20 Minutes," *The Minimalists*, https://www.theminimalists.com/jic/.

Chapter 8

1. Eric Barker, "This Is the Best Way to Overcome Fear of Missing Out," *Time*, June 7, 2016, http://time.com/4358140/overcome-fomo/.
2. Brené Brown. "Brené Brown on Instagram: "#fomokillsmojo"." Instagram. October 15, 2015.
3. Damon Beres, "Heavy Facebook Use Makes Some People Jealous and Depressed: Study," *Huffington Post*, February 4, 2015, http://www.huffingtonpost.com/2015/02/04/facebook-envy_n_6606824.html.
4. Lisa Eadicicco, "Americans Check Their Phones 8 Billion Times a Day," *Time*, December 15, 2015, http://time.com/4147614/smartphone-usage-us-2015/.
5. Evan Asano, "How Much Time Do People Spend on

Social Media?" January 4, 2017. Social Media Today. http://www.socialmediatoday.com/marketing/how-much-time-do-people-spend-social-media-infographic.

6. Thomas Chalmers, *The Expulsive Power of a New Affection* (New York: T.Y. Crowell, 1901).
7. Susan Weinschenk, "Why We're All Addicted to Texts, Twitter and Google," *Psychology Today*, September 11, 2012, https://www.psychologytoday.com/blog/brain-wise/201209/why-were-all-addicted-texts-twitter-and-google.
8. "New Studies Compare Smartphones to Cocaine Addiction," *Elements Behavioral Health*, July 17, 2017, https://www.elementsbehavioralhealth.com/addiction/new-studies-compare-smartphones-cocaine-addiction/.
9. "Oxytocin," *Psychology Today*, https://www.psychologytoday.com/basics/oxytocin.
10. C. S. Lewis, *The Chronicles of Narnia #3: The Horse and His Boy* (New York: HarperTrophy, 1993), 132.

Chapter 9

1. Donald Miller, *Scary Close: Dropping the Act and Finding True Intimacy* (Nashville, TN: Nelson Books, 2015), 225.